5⁰⁰

"They're like cashews, these I-remember-father writings and sayings. . . . Browsers who read one may find themselves unable to stop going on to the next."
—*Booklist*

Bitter or sweet, sentimental or barbed—this compendium of anecdotes, quips, and essays celebrates fathers of all stripes. Highlights include:

- Aissa Wayne's heartfelt account of John Wayne's final, heroic appearance at the Oscars.

- Arthur Marx's recollection of the day his father caught him smoking. Instead of reprimanding him, Groucho gave him a pipe and good tobacco, telling him: "Now you can stop stinking up the house with that cheap stuff."

- Alice Walker's memoir of how her father lovingly urged her always to take her chances with the truth.

- Candice Bergen's deadpan account of umpteen Sunday breakfasts spent sitting on her father's knee next to Charlie McCarthy while the famous ventriloquist merrily squeezed their necks and spoke for both of them.

- Arthur Ashe's remei̵   l triumph over the inj

With charming pen-ai̵
throughout, this marveɪͻus ͻͻͻκ ͻͻͼΐͻ moving and humorous testimony to the enduring legacy of fathers.

JON WINOKUR is the author of *The Portable Curmudgeon, The Portable Curmudgeon Redux, Zen to Go, Mondo Canine,* and other books. He lives in Pacific Palisades, California.

D0973706

FATHERS

Compiled and Edited
by Jon Winokur

A PLUME BOOK

PLUME
Published by the Penguin Group
Penguin Books USA Inc., 375 Hudson Street, New York, New York 10014, U.S.A.
Penguin Books Ltd, 27 Wrights Lane, London W8 5TZ, England
Penguin Books Australia Ltd, Ringwood, Victoria, Australia
Penguin Books Canada Ltd, 10 Alcorn Avenue, Toronto, Ontario, Canada M4V 3B2
Penguin Books (N.Z.) Ltd, 182–190 Wairau Road, Auckland 10, New Zealand

Penguin Books Ltd, Registered Offices: Harmondsworth, Middlesex, England

Published by Plume, an imprint of Dutton Signet, a division of Penguin Books USA Inc.
Previously published in a Dutton edition.

First Plume Printing, June, 1994
10 9 8 7 6 5 4 3 2 1

Copyright © Jon Winokur, 1993
Illustrations copyright © Barbara Kelley, 1993
All rights reserved

 REGISTERED TRADEMARK—MARCA REGISTRADA

LIBRARY OF CONGRESS CATALOGING-IN-PUBLICATION DATA
Fathers / compiled and edited by Jon Winokur.
       p.   cm.
    ISBN 0-452-27207-6
    1. Father and child—Anecdotes.   2. Father and child—Humor.
3. Fathers—Anecdotes.   4. Celebrities—Anecdotes.   5. Fathers in
literature.   I. Winokur, Jon.
HQ755.85.F39   1994
306.874'2—dc20   93–1730
                                                         CIP

Printed in the United States of America
Original hardcover design by Eve L. Kirch

Without limiting the rights under copyright reserved above, no part of this publication
may be reproduced, stored in or introduced into a retrieval system, or transmitted, in any
form, or by any means (electronic, mechanical, photocopying, recording or otherwise),
without the prior written permission of both the copyright owner and the above publisher
of this book.

BOOKS ARE AVAILABLE AT QUANTITY DISCOUNTS WHEN USED TO PROMOTE PRODUCTS OR SERVICES.
FOR INFORMATION PLEASE WRITE TO PREMIUM MARKETING DIVISION, PENGUIN BOOKS USA INC.,
375 HUDSON STREET, NEW YORK, NEW YORK 10014.

For my father

He was a man. Take him for all in all,
I shall not look upon his like again.

WILLIAM SHAKESPEARE, *Hamlet,* Act I, Scene 2

CONTENTS

FATHERS

INTRODUCTION

Even the most wretched among us has a soft spot for his father. Richard Milhous Nixon, "Tricky Dick," one of the most vilified public figures in the history of the United States, living symbol of political chicanery, object of national shame and king of unindicted co-conspirators . . . loved his father. In the course of his rambling, tearful farewell to his White House staff, Nixon spoke lovingly of his parents. After calling his mother a "saint," he spoke of his father: "He was a streetcar motorman first. And then he was a farmer. And then he had a lemon ranch. It was the poorest lemon ranch in California, I can assure you. He sold it before they found oil on it. And then he was a grocer. But he was a great man."

Indeed, your father is a great man whether or not he's a worldly success. He's someone you can look up to. He helps shape your worldview, dispenses discipline, teaches object lessons, hands down material and moral legacies.

1

This collection of the paternal memoirs of promi-
nent people is intended as a celebration of fathers.
There are thumbnail character sketches, quirky rem-
iniscences, and rueful indictments, all in exploration
of the unique bond between father and child. There
are golden moments polished bright over a lifetime
of remembering: Joyce Carol Oates recollects a tran-
scendent flight in a small plane with her father at
the controls, Sean Lennon a ride through Central
Park with his father in a hansom cab. There are
nuggets of fatherly advice: Howard Hughes's father
advised him never to have partners, John F. Kennedy's suggested that he "get laid as often as possible."
There are life lessons (the Mafioso Sam Giancana
taught his daughter never to open the door to a
stranger), and moments of quality time both tradi-
tional and bizarre (Candice Bergen recalls Sunday
morning breakfasts during which she would sit on
her father's knee next to Charlie McCarthy while the
famous ventriloquist merrily squeezed their necks
and spoke for both of them). Men are often defined
in terms of their work, hence the many descriptions
of fathers' occupations (Frank Zappa's was a meteorologist, Harlan Ellison's a dentist who made his
gangster patients check their guns at the door,
George Plimpton's a lawyer who "thought the cornerstone of culture was the mortgage indenture").
There are acts of courage both physical (Yul Brynner stitching a wound to his famous scalp with a
fishhook and nylon line) and moral (Ahmet Ertegun's diplomat father stubbornly defying segregation laws).

In this anthology, assembled from original interviews as well as published sources, I've sought to
highlight the contours of fatherhood without trying
to define it. In a deliberate attempt to be anecdotal

and impressionistic rather than definitive, I have included bits and pieces from novels along with non-fiction material. And although most of it is affectionate, it is not all Norman Rockwell. There are more than a few examples of bad blood (see "Daddy Dearest," page 111, in which Norman Lear declares his father a bigot, Pat Conroy reveals that he always feared his father's fierce temper, and Anatole Broyard laments his father's indifference).

Still, the majority of these excerpts, quotations and essays are fond remembrances. Not necessarily because most of those quoted had *good* fathers, but because, I think, when it comes to remembering a father, memory often yields to idealization and even confabulation. As Nietzsche tells us, if you have not had a good father, it is necessary to invent one. And even if you've had a good father, over the years the line between recollection and invention becomes blurred by wishful thinking, family myth and love.

—J.W.
Pacific Palisades, California
July 1992

Wilfrid Sheed

Fathers

According to our mother you're our father
And that's good enough for us.
　　　　　　　—Harry Ruby, "Father's Day"

I thought at first that I'd made a mistake bringing
my father to America. I was nine years old at the
time and still making mistakes. For one thing, nobody had warned me, before I was stashed away in
a Yank boarding school, that *all* American fathers
were outdoorsmen: that when they weren't hunting
they were fishing, and vice versa, and cooking the
results on a spit.

Now, if there was ever such a thing as a total,
irredeemable indoorsman, it was my father, Frank.
He couldn't fish, because his incessant chatter frightened the fellows away, and no one in his right mind
would have handed him a gun. When he had gone
sailing as a kid, as a young Australian must, he
claimed that he invariably pulled some plug in the
boat which made it sink—a plug no boatsman has
yet been able to identify for me. When absolutely
obliged to throw a ball, he looked as if his arm were
in a splint, and he batted as if he'd just caught something in his eye. In the circumstances, there didn't

4

seem much point in telling my hooligan friends that he was not altogether bad at croquet.

Then there was motor mechanics. If there was one thing American fathers knew about, it was cars, and there was nothing they liked better than lying underneath these things for whole afternoons, tinkering dreamily. In the same situation, my father would undoubtedly have found a hammock and a book while our latest jalopy boiled over unheeded. "Oh Lord, do you suppose we ought to do something?" he would mutter resignedly. "Oh, if we only had a *man,*" my mother would sigh.

Not that we were rich, far from it. In America, we lived in borrowed houses, and in England, Frank had sold our last car for one shilling and sixpence, the equivalent of about thirty cents in uninflated pennies, after ramming into, or being rammed by (who could tell with Frank?), a stray motorcyclist. Still, a man was something we had to send for, since we didn't have one ourselves, every time a door squeaked or a window screen fell out. To this day, I see nothing the least bit funny about light-bulb jokes. All it takes is one Man to change one.

My playmates affected to despise rich kids—it was the Depression, rich kids even despised each other. But we were something infinitely worse than rich: we were intellectual. Nobody else's father had *time* to read books, not with so much fishing still to be done. Books were strictly for women.

So naturally, the next time I saw my father reading, I thought, Why aren't you crocheting or working in lace, or doing something else really manly? I definitely should have been told about this! I would gladly have not learned to read myself and saved everyone the trouble of teaching me; in fact, the worse you read, the higher you stood in my set, the optimum being a complete, stumbling, fur-mouthed halt.

The approach of Visitors Day brought my embarrassment to a veritable Woody Allen crescendo. Why, my mother couldn't even cook, for Pete's sake (although perhaps that's a story for Mother's Day), and they both spoke in rich English accents, which my comrades had drilled me to believe was the fruitiest sound in God's creation. My father would probably say "pip pip" or something and we would just have to run for it. By then the other fathers would have marched in like a Marine platoon, lean and leathery and covered in engine grease, while my father looked for his glasses.

I was actually considering pretending not to know my parents at all, when the other guys' sires began parading around the ring. I stared at them in disbelief. This couldn't be right. For instance, that pipsqueak over there couldn't be Butch Petrillo's dad, could he? Or Slugger Hogan's or Mad Dog Maguire's either. They must have sent substitutes. These fellows looked like bank clerks.

All right, one or two of them looked okay, but some fathers were in even worse shape than mine, and almost all looked older and tireder and manifestly less at ease. Frank's eyes lit with recognition. "Ah, there you are, Wilfrid." Nobody laughed. The egghead sailed through the fishermen like a flagship.

He then proceeded to do the unthinkable: he started a conversation with a son or two *other* than his own. He also talked to their parents, who seemed sincerely grateful; he even made one of them laugh, a brief startled cackle. I won't say that everyone suddenly burst out singing on the lawn, but for a Visitors Day it was almost human. "I think your dad's neat," said Ratso McGonigal, a guy whose pleasure up to then had been imitating my accent. I myself thought that Frank had come through for me quite well. I had made no mistake bringing him over after all.

The above is a composite, verging on myth, of scenes in at least two schools. My father simply felt at home in the world, and he couldn't even see the barbed wire that other people carried around with them for instant installation. The immediate effect on me that day was that I stopped worrying about hunting and fishing for good. Frank looked rosier just lying on his back thinking beautiful thoughts.

The long-range effect was that I started noticing other people's fathers with these glittering standards in mind. In those days, fathers often seemed like space aliens who'd landed inexplicably on their own lawns. "Father is coming home" was usually a signal to get on your horse. "Listen, I'll see you tomorrow," you'd whisper, but too late—already "it" was gallumphing through the door. If it headed for the sofa, you all dispersed to the back yard, like water displaced by a whale. If it disappeared someplace in back, you huddled up front, conscientiously not disturbing it.

The funny thing about these fathers was that, although they seldom expressed anger or much of anything else, everyone seemed terrified of upsetting them. "He's had a hard day." "He works very hard." He was always *explained*. If he seemed to be bouncing off walls tonight or tripping over his tongue, he had been working *very* hard and something truly terrible would happen if you bothered him.

Anyway, Dad broke the day cleanly in two, and God knows what he was like after you'd left. Yet he was always talked about worshipfully. If he offered to take his son and you to a ball game, it was like being promised a private audience with the pope. The privilege brought tears. Never mind that he spent the whole game talking to the guy in the next seat, or simply disappeared for eight innings: from then on, it would always be "Do you remember the time Dad took us to the ball game?"

It was sometimes hard to tell whether fathers enjoyed their isolation or clung to it as a kind of duty. For instance, if there was a singalong around the piano, fathers didn't sing (uncles, maybe). Fathers preferred to sit in the corner talking in low voices about great golf courses they had known. A grown man who sang was nominally encouraged, but it was understood he was playing with the girls.

Back now to my house, where my father is banging the piano dementedly—ragtime, Gilbert and Sullivan, whatever comes out of our bulging piano seat—as if his wrong notes were determined to be heard by the whole village. My friends, future fathers all, stand around in confusion. What kind of guy is this? Is he an Entertainer or something? It is all right to be an Entertainer. But not this stuff.

Yet after a while, they would chirp up shyly. If Mr. Sheed did it, it must be okay—in this house. Fathers were sacred; it was a reciprocal deal. My dad drinks, yours reads books, but they're both dads, aren't they? Frank could recite silly poems in a ripe English accent and they would titter; their *fathers* would titter, if they couldn't make their getaway in time. But *I'd* better not try it.

Thus, fathers when you're small: gray, shadowy men on the edges of rooms, big blustery ones in the middle, but always a space around them like the moats in a zoo. It hardly seemed worth naming a day in their honor.

But then as you got older, they began shyly to beckon you over to their side. The *house* is the enemy, not him, and you're both in this together. Up to now you have been part of the Women and Children, his warders. But now you're big enough to be an apprentice inmate yourself. Obviously, your joint escape must be made through the woods: reluctantly, you talk about hunting and fishing again.

At least the mystery of the out-of-shape sportsman is cleared up. One hunting trip is good for a million words. They plan, buy equipment, look ahead, look behind, but have pathetically little time for the actual thing. Chained to their desks all year, they are considerably more inert than housewives. (At least my father runs for buses. These guys use the car for journeys of over a hundred feet.)

You see less of the American father now, as you enter the great teen-age conspiracy, leaving him more trapped than ever. How you have misjudged this good man. Far from being a tyrant who makes the earth tremble, he is just a run-of-the-mill Noble Savage forced to return to his cage every night, where he reads magazines about hunting and stalking before putting out the cat. When you see him these days, he offers you a beer and says, "Isn't that just like a woman?" every chance he gets. Something about him whispers, Can I join your gang?

The next time you encounter him seriously, it is as the father of a sex object. You knock timidly, as mankind has been doing since it lived in caves, expecting to see the real beast at last, baring his fangs and issuing low growls. But instead he tends to be on your side right away. "Her mother's like that too," he says if the sex bomb doesn't materialize immediately. "It's impossible to get her out of the house." A minute later, he is hollering up the stairs on your behalf. And when she does come down, it is she who gets the orders about being home on time and what not. Something in his tone suggests that taking her out is more trouble than it's worth anyway, that you'd be better off spending the evening with him. Flycasting, no doubt.

How he behaved after the wedding I don't know—I didn't collect enough specimens—but there are precious few father-in-law jokes. So I imagine him holing up with his new son to talk hobbies, which the new son responds to eagerly now, being halfway there himself.

How does all this stack up against my sainted father? Well, for one thing my father never made a joke about women in his life (he never made *any* obvious jokes). He believed that, at least in America, women were slightly brighter than men, a view that may have been the result of meeting too many fathers, those lonesome souls who treated the life of the mind like a social disease.

Frank and I did talk and watch sports a lot together, but only such highly evolved ones as were played with a ball. The crowded stadium, not the primeval forest, was our habitat. And if we knew a female who shared our interest, we were more than pleased to have her along (like many fans, we tended to bore each other from time to time).

Above all, there was no age when one couldn't talk to him. Friends who were as shy around an articulate father as they were around a piano opened up with him. The Miracle of the Loosened Tongues on Visitors Day was repeated at all ages. When the men clustered in defiant bands at one end of the room, Frank might be found at the other, chatting merrily with the women, or outside playing with the children. He seemed the only free soul in a house full of waxworks.

Other people's fathers must have had more to them than they showed to strange children. You sometimes heard them laughing in the next room, though never in this one, where they were usually shielded by a newspaper. There was nothing sissy about reading newspapers, and they would hunker down behind the things for as long as it took, until everyone left and it was safe to come out.

One might suppose these creatures extinct—fathers of one's own age don't seem like that, at least to other grown-ups. But grown-ups never did get quite the view that we did. I do know that when I tried the fathering game myself, I was determined to play it my old man's way, but every instinct in me clamored to reach for that newspaper or disappear into the yard when other people's kids loomed. And I began to think that frolicsome guys like my own father were trying to show me up. A father is not a wind-up toy or an official greeter, by God.

In fact, I found in those years that my father's image clashed frequently with that of his favorite comedian and spitting image, W. C. Fields, the patron saint of other people's fathers. And I suspect that my party trick of singing "The Teddy Bears' Picnic" to any child who would listen, even if I had to strap him in his chair to make him, was simply an unfortunate amalgam of the two styles.

My father's technique was much harder than it looked, like most works of art. But there were two aspects to it that are within reach of any duffer. If a kid was rude to him, he was usually rude right back. ("I wouldn't take that from a grown-up; why should I take it from you?") And he never escaped into heartiness: "Hi, Bill! My son Biff has told me a lot about you," etc. Such indiscriminate babble is almost worse than not talking at all. No fellow human, however small, should be subjected to "How do you like your school, sonny?"

Both principles are the same: you've got your dignity, I've got mine. So far so good. But then what do you *say* to the little so-and-so? That, of course, is where the genius comes in.

LESSONS

My father once attempted to give me a very straight-forward account of the whole reproductive process. He drew two detailed male and female figures and begun explaining the functions of both at length but simply. The diagrams and the unlikely enormity of it all were too much for me. To his amusement, I rushed out of the room to be sick before he was half finished.   JOHN OSBORNE

Back in 1880 when I was a child, I asked my father for a cent. He heard me gravely and then informed me just as gravely that it looked to him as if a Democratic President would be elected that fall, and it behooved every prudent man to exercise especial thrift. Therefore, he would be obliged to deny my request.   CALVIN COOLIDGE

I remember once when I was very young and I was looking at his navel and asked him what that was. And he said, "That's where Custer shot me." Because I knew who Custer was. And I believed that for years—until the point I realized that I had one too, and I didn't get shot.

WILLIAM LEAST HEAT MOON

When I was eighteen I took up smoking a corncob pipe, unbeknown to him. One afternoon, when I was in my bedroom, puffing away on the pipe behind closed doors, I heard the patter of Groucho's little feet approaching down the hallway.

I quickly stowed the pipe, still alight, in the drawer of my desk, and was sitting there with an innocent look on my face when he opened the door and walked in.

He detected the smell of tobacco immediately, and without saying a word turned around and walked back to his room. I was frightened, for I thought perhaps he had gone to get the snake-whip he kept in his closet (for what reason I never have found out). But when he returned he was carrying one of his good Dunhill pipes and a can of tobacco.

"Here," he said, handing me the pipe first, "I think you'll like smoking this better than the cheap corncob you've been using. And here's a can of good tobacco. Now you can stop stinking up the house with that cheap stuff."

"Aren't you angry with me?" I asked.

"What for?" he said. "Smoking won't hurt you as long as you do it in moderation. And that goes for everything else you do, too. I've been smoking since I was seventeen, and except for the fact that I usually feel awful, I'm fit as a fiddle." ARTHUR MARX

I was supposed to become, like him, an "electro-mechanical" engineer—in reality he was the smallest independent elevator contractor in the business—and drive around in a car linked to his by radio. His great concern was to guard me against the perils of the profession. His favorite teaching method was the Horrible Example.

Walking through a clangorous steel-fabricating shed, he would point to a wall and say, "See that red stain, Al? That was Jimmy Flaherty. He bent over that little motor-generator set and caught his sleeve on the shaft. By the time we got him out, he was just a red rag."

Such stories were supposed to protect me from danger; actually, they made me dread the day when I would have to contend with those intimidating machines. ALBERT GOLDMAN

Father thought a day out huntin' taught you much more than a day at school. DICK FRANCIS

My father taught me to notice things. One day, I was playing with an "express wagon," a little wagon with a railing around it. It had a ball in it, and when I pulled the wagon, I noticed something about the way the ball moved. I went to my father and said,

"Say, Pop, I noticed something. When I pull the wagon, the ball rolls to the back of the wagon. And when I'm pulling it along and I suddenly stop, the ball rolls to the front of the wagon. Why is that?"

"That nobody knows," he said. "The general principle is that things which are moving tend to keep on moving, and things which are standing still tend to stand still, unless you push them hard. This tendency is called 'inertia,' but nobody knows why it's true." Now, that's a deep understanding. He didn't just give me the name.

He went on to say, "If you look from the side, you'll see that it's the back of the wagon that you're pulling against the ball, and the ball stands still. As a matter of fact, from the friction it starts to move forward a little bit in relation to the ground. It doesn't move back."

I ran back to the little wagon and set the ball up again and pulled the wagon. Looking sideways, I saw that indeed he was right. Relative to the sidewalk, it moved forward a little bit.

That's the way I was educated by my father, with those kinds of examples and discussions: no pressure—just lovely, interesting discussions. It has motivated me for the rest of my life, and makes me interested in *all* the sciences. (It just happens I do physics better.) RICHARD P. FEYNMAN

When I was a child, my father taught me to put up my fists like a boy and to be prepared to defend myself at all times. CAMILLE PAGLIA

I was nine years old. I was very skinny and not at all strong. There was a karate club very close to my home, and my father brought me there. I fell in love with karate right away and started going there every day. I had a great teacher, and I loved all the running and jumping and stretching. My father is wonderful, a very, very smart man. He knew that karate was not only physical—it also builds your mental attitude.   JEAN-CLAUDE VAN DAMME

When I was fifteen years old I was playing with my father and I hit an eight-iron into a trap, and the club went right into the trap after the ball. My father said, "Young man, that'll be the last club you'll throw or the last hole you'll play if I have anything to say about it." He got his message across.

JACK NICKLAUS

I hit my first tennis ball when I was six. We lived two doors from a playground in Cincinnati and we had no money, my dad had gone through the Depression. I guess I threw a racket over the fence or something when I was seven. You know how you can feel eyes on you? I looked around and he was at the other end of the court with his fingers in the chain-link fence and he sort of motioned me to come toward him. That was probably the longest walk I've ever made in my life. He said (this is 1937), "If I ever see you do that again, I'll drop you like a hot potato." I never threw a racket again.

TONY TRABERT

My father told me that I was able to walk when I was only six months old. And wouldn't you know it, he got me walking after a baseball. Getting a baseball was just about the first thing I was able to do. He put two chairs close to each other and then put a baseball on one. I was clinging to the other. He walked me through two or three times. "See the ball," he said. "See the ball." Then he turned me loose—and I went for the ball myself. When he knew I could chase a ball, he gave me batting lessons. He handed me a rubber ball and a little stick maybe two feet long, and sat me in the middle of the floor. I'd play with the ball all day long, hitting it with the stick, then crawling or toddling after it across the room. My dad was determined that if I wanted to, I would become a baseball player and not end up in the steel mills the way he did.

WILLIE MAYS

My father never gave me, by fire or water, a baptism into publishing; he wasn't a baptising type. He adopted the sink-or-swim method, so the first weeks I was at Scribners, in 1946, my assignment was to deal with Ernest Hemingway.

CHARLES SCRIBNER, JR.

I lived with my father only six years, the first six years of my life, but I remember vividly so many of his characteristics, and I still find myself emulating them. My mother taught me my ABCs. From my father I learned the glories of going to the bathroom outside.

LEWIS GRIZZARD

One summer I made $50 a week, and my father charged me $25 a week rent. I asked him if that wasn't a little high. He said that if I could do better than that for food and lodging seven days a week I could move out.

TED TURNER

To impress upon us what the loss of the soul through mortal sin meant, my father would light a match, grab our hands and hold them briefly over the flame, saying: "See how that feels? Now imagine that for all eternity."   PAT BUCHANAN

Although he didn't talk a lot, over the years I became aware by osmosis of his values. As a child growing up in the hills of Los Angeles, going to a private school, I was sheltered. It wasn't until the family moved to the East Coast, when Dad played on Broadway in *Mr. Roberts*, that I became aware of racism. That was where I first heard schoolmates use the word *nigger*. One day my father was driving me to the movies, and I used the word myself. He stopped the car, turned to me and smacked me across the face.   JANE FONDA

One night at about two o'clock in the morning my father caught a man stealing bananas from our backyard. He went over to the man with his machete, took the bananas, cut the bunch in half and said, "Here, you can have it." And then he said, "From now on, if you need anything from the back of our house, come to the front."

JUAN "CHI CHI" RODRIGUEZ

He had a pretty fearful death, the result of years of dissipation and self-abuse, and in those few days it seemed to me he coughed up most of his lungs and stomach. He died in a Catholic hospital. At the end of his ward was a chapel where the sisters said their offices every couple of hours. Just before he died he was received into the Roman Catholic church. When I visited him the last night, he gave me a little self-conscious and half-conscious speech about the evils of overindulgence in food, alcohol, games of chance, and commercial sex. One of the last things he said was the old gag that he was dying of fast women, slow horses, crooked cards, and straight whiskey. I have never been a heavy drinker and I have never had the slightest interest in any form of gambling. Sex and food I have managed to cope with.

KENNETH REXROTH

I recall a scene when I was only three or so in which my father questioned me about a fruit jar I had accidentally broken. I felt he knew I had broken it, at the same time I couldn't be sure. Apparently breaking it was, in any event, the wrong thing to have done. I could say, Yes, I broke the jar, and risk a whipping for breaking something valuable, or No, I did not break it, and perhaps bluff my way through.

I've never forgotten my feeling that he really wanted me to tell the truth. And because he seemed to desire it—and the moments during which he waited for my reply seemed quite out of time, so much so I can still feel them, and, as I said, I was only three—I confessed. I broke the jar, I said. I think he hugged me. He probably didn't, but I still feel as if he did, so embraced did I feel by the happy

relief I noted on his face and by the fact that he
didn't punish me at all, but seemed, instead, pleased
with me. I think it was at that moment that I resolved to take my chances with the truth, although
as the years rolled on I was to break more serious
things in his scheme of things than fruit jars.

ALICE WALKER

When I was about five years old my father, happen-
ing to look into the fire, spied in the middle of those
most burning flames, a little creature like a lizard,
which was sporting in the core of the most intense
flames. Pointing it out, he gave me a great box on
the ear, which caused me to howl and weep with all
my might. Then he pacified me good-humoredly
and spoke as follows; "My dear little boy, I am not
striking you for any wrong you may have done, but
only to make you remember that the lizard which
you see in the fire is a salamander, a creature which
has never been seen before by anyone of whom we
have creditable information." So saying he kissed me
and gave me some pieces of money.

BENVENUTO CELLINI

He was a lone "general practitioner." He never had
a partner (my mother never would have tolerated
it!), but through his office came a stream of young
lawyers just out of law school whom he trained in
the old apprentice style. They adored him, but
found him difficult to work for. Many of them became district attorneys and judges, or founded prosperous law firms that far outshone him. He had his
own way—his *very* own way—of doing everything.
This included the way you use an index, the way

you hold a pen, the way you talk to clients. Each of these apprentices stayed for a few years and then went on—much wiser in the law and how to practice it, but relieved at not being told how to do everything. I personally suffered more than once from my father's insistence on doing things his way. After I had been shaving for many years my father still insisted on my running the razor *against* the grain of my facial hair, as "the only way to get a close shave." His golf lessons, offered in a warm spirit of paternal helpfulness, made me hate the game, and I've never gone near a golf course since.

DANIEL J. BOORSTIN

When my father was not in consultation with a patient, I would haunt his office, careful not to disturb his work. It was quite a serious place, a great wonder to me as a child, lined with books that provoked my curiosity. It felt different from any room I had ever been in. I remember standing on a great pile of books to reach the height of my father's desk. He showed me a glass slide on which he had placed a drop of water. He held the slide in his hand between his thumb and index finger and said, "Martha, what do you see?" I said, simply enough, "Water." And he said, "Pure water?" I said, "I think so. Pure water." I thought my father was acting a bit strange and I did not know what he was getting at. Then, from a high shelf over his desk, he removed a microscope and placed it near me. He adjusted the window shade to give the moment the proper light and placed the slide of water on his microscope. I squinted one eye closed and brought the other to the heavy black lens. Then I saw the contents of the slide of water and said to my father in horror, "But there are wiggles in it!" He said, "Yes, it is impure. Just remember this all your life, Martha. You must look for the truth." Look for the truth, whatever that truth may be—good, bad, or unsettling.

I have never forgotten the vividness of that moment, which has presided like a star over my life. In a curious way, this was my first dance lesson—a gesture toward the truth. MARTHA GRAHAM

In April of 1951 I was ten years old and living with my family on Chicago's South Side when the newspapers reported that General of the Army Douglas MacArthur was to be paraded past our neighborhood as part of the clamorous tour of American cities that followed his recall from Korea. The news put my father in a quandary. He knew that MacArthur represented a big part of our history and that it would be wrong to deny me a look at him. But he also saw MacArthur's dismissal not as the tragedy the general and his admirers believed it to be but as the most forceful evidence that the Constitution still mattered, that it was incumbent upon even the most exalted soldier to follow the orders of his civilian commander in chief.

My clearest memories of that day are not of the parade but of my father walking with me across the grassy Midway, gravely explaining why, while it was okay for us to have a glimpse of the general, we wouldn't be sharing in the wild enthusiasm the crowds were sure to show. A mighty cheer went up as, first, police motorcycles appeared, and then the big open car in which the general sat. My father did not cheer, and so, of course, neither did I.

GEOFFREY C. WARD

[My father] taught me how to print my name, and devised a way to teach me how to write in script. In the early hours of the morning after he got home from work, he sat at the kitchen table laboriously dotting out my name over and over in a drugstore tablet. I spent the next several days tracing the dots until I was able to sign myself with a fairly respectable flourish.

FLORENCE KING

We had to have our bagpipe lessons every Sunday and then we got our allowance. There was a very clear connection of doing what we had to do before we got paid.

TIMOTHY FORBES of his father, Malcolm S. Forbes

I learned from the example of my father that the manner in which one endures what must be endured is more important than the thing that must be endured.

DEAN ACHESON

My father was an avid gardener. On many a summer morning he rousted me out of bed well before sunup and handed me a hoe. We had more than an acre to tend, and the objective was to get as much as possible done before the sun got too high in the sky and the temperature rose above 100. The humidity in that region, while good for the skin and for growing vegetables, is oppressive, and heat exhaustion is always a possibility in summer. On several occasions my thoughts turned patricidal. But as the years have passed, I have grown to appreciate what my dad taught me, not only about growing things in the earth but also about responsibility and the value of hard, physical work. I now derive physical and spiritual pleasure from gardening. All this galls me a little, because my dad always said it would turn out this way.   DON HENLEY

Yul delighted in burning the candle at both ends. No matter how much of a nightlife he was living, he maintained our ritual of early breakfast. When I awoke, I would pad out to the kitchen or dining room to join him, and there he would stand in a silk kimono, grilling a couple of steaks on the very latest kitchen appliance—he loved modern appliances of all kinds. The steaks were for him, of course. I just had cereal. We read the paper together (even before I could really read), watched Dave Garroway, and savored the morning as the familiar wake-up smells of coffee, cigarettes and grilled sirloin made the day begin. All this transpired without a word between us. The rest of the day might have been filled with conversation, but breakfast was a sacred, silent ritual, a building block in the larger lesson Yul was trying to teach his son: the value of rituals.

          ROCK BRYNNER of his father, Yul Brynner

I was a little more than four years old when Sam decided the family needed a vacation in Rhinelander, Wisconsin. . . .

It turned out to be a wonderful time, with Sam and Momma taking me shopping, swimming together at an almost private beach, and picnicking, something I had never done before. It was a happy time and I tried my damnedest to please.

Life seemed so free and easy that I was totally unaware of any danger that might be present. Of course, at that age I knew nothing of Sam's operating a still, or being involved in robberies, or of any criminal activity of any kind.

Danger was the furthest thing from my mind when late one Saturday morning I heard a knock at the door of our suite. Momma and Dad were still in their bedroom and Bonnie was playing in the playpen in our bedroom. There was a second knock followed by a man's voice on the other side of the door announcing rather cheerfully, "Breakfast is served." Without further thought, I went straight to the door, opened it, and let the man wheel the table of food into the main sitting room. As the waiter set the table, Sam came into the room from his bedroom. For an instant, he turned white as a sheet. He ducked back into his room and returned with my mother to pay the waiter.

Almost before the door had been closed by the waiter, Sam was raging.

"Never, never open the door to a stranger again!" he shouted. He upended me and gave me a thorough spanking to bring the lesson home. Then he stalked off without eating, mumbling something about how I was going to "get us all killed one day."

ANTOINETTE GIANCANA

I never fully understood what was my father's reason for purposely exposing me to various forms of primitive religious excesses, although later I assumed that what he had in mind was to discourage me from being captivated by such exhibitions. But expose me he did even though he never once proposed that I attend his own church services.

Instead, my father often suggested that I might be interested in going with him to remote parts of Jefferson, Burke, and Richmond counties to witness foot-washing services, a clay-eating communion ritual, a coming-through orgy, a snake-handling performance, or an emotion-charged glossolalia and unknown-tongue spectacle. It was my assumption on many occasions that my father hoped that my reaction would result in my being spared, at some time in the future, the indignity of indulging in the absurd.   ERSKINE CALDWELL

When we got to the range, I was given cotton to muffle the sound of the pistol fire, but I held my hands over my ears anyway while my father and the other shooters fired round after round into the rectangular targets. As my father shot, the other marines gathered to watch him, and I noted that the .45-caliber pistol jumped in his hand each time he squeezed the trigger. After he had finished, he reloaded his weapon, placed me on the firing line, and instructed me to hold it tightly with both hands. Anticipating a kick similar to that of my rifle, I squeezed off a round and was dismayed that the weapon jumped from my hands and struck me in the eye.

Stung by the blow from the pistol and embarrassed by my own ineptitude, I wanted to cry, but before I could vent my tears, my father had placed the .45 back in my hands. He then steadied my hands with his own, and together we fired the remaining rounds from the ammunition clip. After we had finished, I was given the task of policing the area of spent cartridges, and for the rest of the afternoon I was kidded about the mouse on my right eye. Later I had time to reflect on my growing respect for handguns, but for most of the ride home I was preoccupied with the newly acquired awareness that a boy did not cry in the presence of grown men.   LEWIS B. PULLER, JR.

I learned from my father how to work. I learned from him that work is life and life is work, and work is hard.   PHILIP ROTH

The lease said about I and my fathers trip from the Bureau of Manhattan to our new home the soonest mended. In some way ether I or he got balled up on the grand concorpse and the next thing you know we was thretning to swoop down on Pittsfield. Are you lost daddy I arsked tenderly. Shut up he explained.

RING LARDNER, "The Young Immigrants"

Allen Wheelis

Grass

It was the last day of school. The report cards had
been distributed, and—to my great relief—I had
passed. Now at eleven o'clock in the morning I was on
my way home with two friends. We felt exhilaration
at the prospect of three months of freedom and mani-
fested it by pushing each other, yelling, throwing rocks
at a bottle, chasing a grass snake, and rolling a log into
the creek. Being eight years old, it took us a long time
to reach our homes. Before parting we made plans to
meet that afternoon to play ball. I ran through the tall
grass up to the back door and into the kitchen. My
mother was stirring something on the stove.

"Mama, I passed!"

"Not so loud, hon." She leaned over and kissed
me, then looked at the report card. "This is very
good. Show it to Daddy if he's not asleep."

I went through the bedroom to the glassed-in
porch where my father lay sick with tuberculosis.
The bed faced away from the door and I could not
tell whether he was asleep or not.

"Daddy?"

"Come in, son."

"I passed," I said, offering the card.

He smiled and I lowered my eyes. I could never bring myself to face for long the level gaze of those pale blue eyes which seemed effortlessly to read my mind. He looked over the report. "I see you got seventy-five in conduct."

"Yes, sir."

"Do you have an explanation?"

"No, sir."

"Do you think you deserved a better grade?"

"No . . . sir."

"Then you *do* have an explanation?"

I twisted one foot around the other. "Yes, sir. I guess so, sir."

"What is the explanation?"

This tireless interrogation could, I knew, be carried on for hours. Mumbling the words, I began to recount my sins. "I guess I . . . talked too much."

"Speak up, son."

"Yes, sir. I talked too much . . . and laughed . . . and cut up."

"Do you find silence so difficult?"

"Sir?"

"Was it so hard to be quiet?"

"Yes . . . sir. I guess so."

"You don't seem to find it difficult now."

I looked up and found him smiling. It wasn't going to be so bad after all. "But the other grades are good," he said. I grinned and turned to look out the window. Heat waves shimmered over the tin roof of the barn; away to the west was an unbroken field of sunflowers. Everything was bathed in, and seemed to be made drowsy by, the hot, bright sunlight. I thought of playing ball and wished dinner were over so I could go now. "Daddy, can I go over to Paul's house after dinner?" Almost before the words were out I realized my mistake. I should have asked my mother first. She might have said yes without consulting my father.

"No. You have to work, son."

"What've I got to do?"

He looked out over the several acres which we called the back yard. "You have to cut the grass."

Through a long wet spring the grass had sprung up until it was nearly a foot high. Now, in June, the rain was over and the heat was beginning to turn the grass brown. As we had no lawn mower, any cutting of grass or weeds was done by hoe, scythe, or sickle. It was with one of these I assumed the grass would be cut, but I was mistaken. After dinner my father gave me directions. The tool was to be an old, ivory-handled, straight-edge razor. The method was to grasp a handful of grass in the left hand and cut it level with the ground with the razor. The grass was to be put in a basket, along with any rocks or sticks that might be found on the ground. When the basket was full it was to be removed some hundred yards where the grass could be emptied and burned. When the razor was dull it was to be sharpened on a whetstone in the barn.

I changed my clothes, put on a straw hat, and went to work. Unable to realize the extent of the task or to gauge the time required, my only thought was to finish as soon as possible so as to be able to play before the afternoon was over. I began in the center of the yard and could see my father watching from his bed on the porch. After a few experimental slashes an idea occurred to me. I walked to the house and stood under the windows of the porch.

"Daddy."

"Yes, son."

"When I've finished can I play baseball?"

"Yes."

I resumed work, thinking I would cut fast and get it over in a couple of hours. For a few minutes all went well; there was some satisfaction in watching the thin steel cut easily through dry grass. I grabbed big handfuls and hacked away with gusto. Soon my father called. Obediently I walked to the porch. "Yes, sir?" He was looking through field glasses at the small patch of ground that had been cleared.

"Son, I want you to cut the grass *level* with the ground. Therefore you will have to cut slower and more carefully. Take a smaller handful at a time so you can cut it evenly. Also, you must pick up every stone." This referred to the few pebbles left in the cleared area. "Do you understand?"

"Yes, sir."

"Now go back and do that patch over again, and cut it level with the ground."

"Yes, sir."

Walking back I wondered why I had not started in some part of the yard out of my father's view. The work was now harder; for the stubble was only one or two inches high and was difficult to hold while being cut. It took an hour to do again the area originally cleared in a few minutes. By this time I was tired and disheartened. Sweat ran down my forehead and into my eyes; my mouth was dry. The razor could not be held by the handle, for the blade would fold back. It had to be held by its narrow shank which already had raised a blister. Presently I heard my friends; soon they came into view and approached the fence.

"Whatya doin'?"

"Cuttin' the grass."

"What's that you're cuttin' it with?"

"A razor."

They laughed. "That's a funny thing to be cuttin' grass with."

"Son!" The boys stopped laughing and I went to the porch.

"Yes, sir?"

"If you want to talk to your friends, you may; but don't stop working while you talk."

"Yes, sir." I went back to the basket and resumed cutting.

"What'd he say?" Paul asked in a lowered voice.

"He said I had to work."

"You cain't play ball?"

"No."

"How long is he going to make you work?"

"I don't know."

"Well . . . I guess we might as well go on."

I looked up with longing. They were standing outside the fence, poking their toes idly through the palings. James was rhythmically pounding his fist into the socket of a first baseman's mitt.

"Yeah, let's get goin'."

"Can you get away later on?" Paul asked.

"Maybe I can. I'll try. I'll see if he'll let me." The two boys began to wander off. "I'll try to come later," I called urgently, hoping my father would not hear.

When they were gone I tried for a while to cut faster, but my hand hurt. Several times I had struck rocks with the razor, and the blade was getting dull. Gingerly I got up from my sore knees, went to the hydrant, allowed the water to run until cool, and drank from my cupped hands. Then I went to the barn and began whetting the blade on the stone. When it was sharp I sat down to rest. Being out of my father's sight I felt relatively secure for the moment. The chinaberry tree cast a liquid pattern of sun and shadow before the door. The berries were green and firm, just right for a slingshot.

"Son!"

With a sense of guilt I hurried to my father's window. "Yes, sir."

"Get back to work. It's not time to rest yet."

At midafternoon I looked about and saw how little I had done. Heat waves shimmered before my eyes and I realized that I would not finish today and perhaps not tomorrow. Leaving the razor on the ground, I made the familiar trek to my father's window.

"Daddy."

"Yes."

"Can I quit now?"

"No, son."

"I cain't finish it this afternoon."

"I know."

"Then cain't I go play ball now and finish it tomorrow?"

"No."

"When can I play ball?"

"When you have finished cutting the grass."

"How long do you think it'll take me?"

"Two or three months."

"Well, can . . . ?"

"Now that's enough. Go back to work."

I resumed work at a sullenly slow pace. To spare my knees I sat down, cutting around me as far as I could reach, then moving to a new place and sitting down again.

"Son!"

I went back to the porch. "Yes, sir."

"Do you want to be a lazy, no-account scoundrel?"
The voice was harsh and angry.

"No, sir."

"Then don't you ever let me see you sitting down
to work again! Now you get back there as quick as
you can and stand on your knees."

The afternoon wore on with excruciating slow-
ness. The sun gradually declined. The thin shank of
the razor cut into my hand and the blisters broke. I
showed them to my father, hoping they would prove
incapacitating, but he bandaged them and sent me
back. Near sundown I heard the sounds of my
friends returning to their homes, but they did not
come by to talk. Finally my mother came to the back
door, said supper was ready. The day's work was
over.

When I woke the next morning I thought it was
another school day, then remembered the preceding
afternoon and knew that school was far better than
cutting grass. I knew that my father intended for
me to continue the work, but as no specific order
had been given for this particular day there was possibility of escape. I decided to ask my mother for
permission to play and be gone before my father
realized what had happened. My mother was cooking breakfast when I finished dressing. I made myself useful and waited until, for some reason, she
went on the back porch. Now we were separated
from my father by four rooms and clearly out of
earshot.

"Mama, can I go over to Paul's house?"

"Why yes, hon, I guess so."

That was my mother. To the reasonable request
she said yes immediately; the unreasonable required
a varying amount of cajolery, but in the end that,

too, would be granted. When breakfast was over, I quickly got my cap, whispered a soft good-bye, and started out. I had reached the back door when she called. "Be sure you come back before dinner."

"Son!"

I stopped. In another moment I would have been far enough away to pretend I had not heard. But though my conscience might be deaf to a small voice, it was not deaf to this sternly audible one. If I ran now I would never be able to look at my father and say, "No, I didn't hear you." I gave my mother a reproachful glance as I went back through the kitchen. "Now I won't get to go," I said darkly.

I entered the glass porch and stood by the bed, eyes lowered. I was aware of omitting the required "Yes, sir," but did not care.

"Where were you off to?"

"To Paul's."

"Who told you you could go?"

"Mama."

"Did you ask her?"

"Yes."

"Yes *what?*"

"Yes, sir," I said sulkily.

"Didn't you know I wanted you to work today?"

"No, sir."

"Don't you remember my telling you that you could not play until you finished cutting the grass?"

"No, sir." One lie followed another now. "Anyway . . . that will take just about . . . all summer." My mouth was dry and I was swallowing heavily. "James and Paul . . . don't have to work and . . . I don't see why . . . I . . . have to work all the time."

I choked, my eyes burned, and tears were just one harsh word away. After a moment I saw the covers of the bed move; my father's long, wasted legs appeared. The tears broke, flooding my face. My father stood up, slowly, with difficulty, found his slippers, and put on a bathrobe. My ear was seized and twisted by a bony hand, and I was propelled into the bathroom. My father sat on the edge of the tub and held me in front of him. The fingers were relentless, and it seemed that my ear would be torn from my head.

"Look at me, son."

Tears were dripping from my chin, and every other moment my chest was convulsed by a rattling inspiration. Trying to stop crying, I managed at last to raise my head and look in my father's face. The head and neck were thin. The skin had a grayish glint, and the lines that ran down from his nose were straight. His eyes were steady, and on their level, searching gaze my conscience was impaled.

"Do you know why you are going to be punished?"

The pose of injured innocence was gone now. My guilt seemed everywhere, there was no place to hide.

"Yes . . . sir."

"Why?"

"Because . . . I . . . didn't tell the . . . truth." It was terrible to look into those eyes.

"And?" The question was clipped and hard.

"And . . . because . . . ."

I tried to search my conscience and enumerate my sins, but my mind was a shambles and my past was mountainous with guilt. I could not speak. My eyes dropped.

"Look at me, son."

It was agony to lift my eyes again to that knifelike gaze, that implacable accusation.

"You are being punished because you tried to get your mother's permission for an act you knew to be wrong. You were scoundrel enough to do that!" the razored voice said. "Do you understand?"

"Yes . . . sir."

"You are being punished, further, because you were sullen and insubordinate. Do you understand?"

"Yes . . . sir."

I saw the other hand move and felt the old, sick terror. The hand grasped the clothes of my back and lifted me onto my father's knees. My head hung down to the floor. The hand began to rise and fall.

"Do you understand why you're being punished?"

"Ye . . . es . . . sir."

The blows were heavy and I cried.

"Will you ever do any of those things again?"

"No . . . sir."

The whipping lasted about a minute, after which I was placed on my feet. "Now, stop crying and wash your face. Then go out in the yard to work."

Still sobbing, I approached the lavatory, turned on a trickle of water. Behind me I heard my father stand and slowly leave the room. I held both hands under the faucet, stared with unseeing eyes at the drops of water tumbling over my fingers. Gradually the sobs diminished. I washed my face and left the room, closing the door softly. Passing through the kitchen I was aware that my mother was looking at me with compassion, but I avoided her eyes. To look at her now would be to cry again.

All that day I worked steadily and quietly, asked no questions, made no requests. The work was an expiation and my father found no occasion to criticize. Several times my mother brought out something cold for me to drink. She did not mention my punishment but knowledge of it was eloquent in her eyes. In the afternoon I began to feel better and thought of my friends and of playing ball.

Knowing it to be out of the question, I only dreamed about it.

That evening when supper was over and the dishes washed my father called me.

"Tell him you're sorry," my mother whispered.

In our house after every punishment there had to be a reconciliation, the integrity of the bonds that held us had to be reaffirmed. Words of understanding had to be spoken, tokens of love given and received. I walked out on the porch. The sky was filled with masses of purple and red.

"Do you feel better now, son?"

"Yes, sir." The blue eyes contained a reflection of the sunset. "I'm sorry I acted the way I did this morning."

A hand was laid on my head. "You said you didn't know why you had to work, didn't you?"

"Yes, sir, but I . . ."

"That's all right, son. I'll tell you. You ought to know. When you are grown you will have to work to make a living. All your life you'll have to work. Even if we were rich you would labor, because idleness is sinful. The Bible tells us that. I hope some day you will be able to work with your head, but first you've got to know how to work with your hands." The color of the ponderous clouds was deepening to blue and black. "No one is born knowing how to work. It is something we have to learn. You've got to learn to set your mind to a job and keep at it, no matter how hard it is or how long it takes or how much you dislike it. If you don't learn that you'll never amount to anything. And this is the time to learn it. Now do you know why you have to cut the grass?"

"Yes, sir."

"I don't like to make you work when you want to

play, but it's for your own good. Can you understand that?"

"Yes, sir."

"Will you be a good boy and work hard this summer until the job is done?"

"Yes, sir."

I left the room feeling better. It was good to be
forgiven, to be on good terms with one's father.

Day after day I worked in the yard, standing on
my knees, cutting the grass close to the ground.
There were few interruptions to break the monot-
ony. Three or four times a day I went to the barn
and sharpened the razor, but these trips were no
escape. If I went too often or stayed too long my
father took notice and put a stop to it. Many times
each day I carried away the full basket of grass and
stones, but the times of my departure and return
were always observed. No evasions were possible because nothing escaped my father's eyes.

One day in July at noon I heard a rattle of dishes
indicating that the table was being set. I was hot and
tired and thirsty. I could smell the dinner cooking
and thought of the tall glasses of iced tea. My
mother came to the back door. At first I thought it
was to call me, but it was only to throw out dishwa-
ter. Suddenly I dropped the razor and ran to the
back steps.

"Mama," I called eagerly, but not loud enough for
my father to hear. "Is dinner ready?"

"Yes, hon."

I came in, washed my hands, sat in the kitchen to
wait.

"Son!"

It was my father's voice, the everlasting surveil-
lance I could never escape.

"Yes, sir."

"What did you come in for?"

"Mama said dinner was ready."

"Did you *ask* her?"

"Yes, sir."

"You trifling scoundrel! Get on back outside to work! And wait till she *calls* you to dinner! You understand?"

As weeks passed the heat increased and the grass withered. Had a match been touched to it the work of a summer would have been accomplished in a few minutes. No rain fell, even for a day, to interrupt the work. The grass did not grow, and the ground which was cleared on the first day remained bare. The earth was baked to a depth of four or five feet and began to crack. The only living thing I encountered was an occasional spider climbing desperately in or out of the crevices in search of a habitable place. My friends knew I had to work and no longer came looking for me. Occasionally I would hear them playing in a nearby field, and sometimes in the mornings would see them pass with fishing poles over their shoulders. I knew that I was not missed, that they had stopped thinking of me and probably did not mention my name.

I became inured to the work but not reconciled to it, and throughout the summer continued to resist. Whippings—which had been rare before—were now common, and after each I would, in the evening, be required to apologize. I would go out on my father's glass porch, say I was sorry, and listen guiltily to a restatement of the principles involved. Tirelessly my father would explain what I had done wrong, the importance of learning to work, and the benefit to my character which this discipline would eventually bring about. After each of these sessions I would feel that I was innately lazy, unworthy, and impulsive. Each time I would resolve to try harder, to overcome my resentment, but each time would relapse. After two or three days I would again become sullen or rebellious and again would be punished. Sometimes I saw my mother in tears and knew she interceded in my behalf, but her efforts were ineffective.

Throughout June and July I worked every day except Sundays. As the job seemed endless I made no future plans. Anything that would last all summer was too large an obstacle to plan beyond, any happiness which lay at its end too remote to lift my spirit. About the middle of August, however, my outlook changed. One evening at sundown I noticed that relatively little grass remained standing. For the first time since the beginning of summer I realized that the job would have an end, that I would be free. Surveying the area remaining to be cut, I attempted to divide it by the area which could be cleared in a single day and reached an estimate of five days. I felt a surge of hope and began visualizing what I would do when I was through. During the next several days I worked faster and more willingly, but found that I had been too sanguine in my estimate. I did not finish on the fifth day or the sixth. But on the evening of the seventh it was apparent to my father as well as to me that the next day the job would be done. Only one or two hours of work remained.

The following morning—for the first time since May—I woke to the sound of rain. I wanted to work anyway, to get it over, but was told I could not. Then I asked if I could go to Paul's house to play until the rain stopped. Again the answer was no. About nine o'clock the rain let up and I hurriedly began to work, but the lull was brief and after a few minutes I had to stop. I stood under the awning which extended out over the windows of my father's porch and waited. After a while I sat on the ground and leaned against the house. A half hour passed. The rain was steady now, seemingly would last all day. It dripped continuously from the canvas and formed a little trench in the earth in front of my feet. I stared out at the gray sky in a dull trance.

"I wish I could go to Paul's house."

I spoke in a low, sullen voice, hardly knowing whether I was talking to myself or to my father.

"It's not fair not to let me play . . . just because it's raining. It's not fair at all."

There was no comment from above. Minutes passed.

"You're a mean bastard!"

A feeling of strangeness swept over me. I had never cursed, was not used to such words. Something violent was stirring in me, something long stifled was rankling for expression.

"If you think you can kick me around all the time you're wrong . . . you damned old bastard!"

At any moment I expected to be called. I would go inside then and receive a whipping worse than I had known possible. A minute passed in silence.

Could it be that my father had not heard? That seemed unlikely, for always I spoke from this place and was always heard. The windows were open. There was nothing to prevent his hearing. Oh he had heard, all right. I was sure of that. Still, why wasn't I called? The waiting began to get on my nerves. Feeling that I could not make matters worse, I continued. This time I spoke louder and more viciously.

"You're the meanest man in the world. You lie up there in bed and are mean to everybody. I hate you!"

I began to feel astonished at myself. How incredible that I should be saying such things—I who had never dared a word of disrespect!

But why didn't he call? What was he waiting for? Was he waiting for me to say my worst so as to be able to whip me all the harder? The rain drizzled down. The day was gray and quiet. The whole thing began to seem unreal. The absence of reaction was as incredible as the defamation. Both seemed impossible. It was like a bad dream.

But it's real! I thought furiously. I *had* said those things, and would keep on saying them till I made him answer. I became frantic, poured out a tirade of abuse, searched my memory for every dirty word I knew, and when the store of profanity was exhausted and I stopped, breathless, to listen . . . there was no response.

"You goddamn dirty son of a bitch!" I screamed, "I wish you was dead! I wish you was dead, do you hear? Do you hear me?"

I had finished. Now something would happen. I cowered and waited for it, but there was no word from the porch. Not a sound. Not even the stir of bedclothes.

The rage passed and I became miserable. I sat with arms around my knees, staring blankly at the indifferent rain. As the minutes went by I became more appalled by what I had done. Its meaning broadened, expanded in endless ramifications, became boundless and unforgivable. I had broken the commandment to honor thy father and mother. I had taken the name of the Lord in vain, and that was the same as cursing God. I thought of my mother. What would she say when she learned? I pictured her face. She would cry.

For another half hour I sat there. I no longer expected to be called. For some reason the matter was to be left in abeyance. Finally, unable to endure further waiting, I got up and walked away. I went to the barn and wandered about morosely, expecting momentarily to see my mother enter to say that my father wanted me, but she did not come, and the morning passed without further incident.

On entering the house for dinner my first concern was to learn whether she knew. When she smiled I knew that she did not. Now that I was indoors I knew something would happen. I stayed as far from the porch as possible and spoke in low tones. Yet my father must know me to be present. I could not eat, and soon left the house and went back to the barn, where I felt somewhat less vulnerable.

I spent the afternoon there alone, sitting on a box, waiting. Occasionally I would get up and walk around aimlessly. Sometimes I would stand in the doorway looking out at the rain. Though unrestrained I felt myself a prisoner. I searched through my small understanding of my father but found no explanation of the delay. It was unlike him to postpone a whipping. Then it occurred to me that what I had done might so far exceed ordinary transgression as to require a special punishment. Perhaps I would not be whipped at all but sent away from home, never be permitted to come back.

When supper time came I sneaked into the house and tried to be inconspicuous, but was so agitated that my mother was concerned. She looked at me inquiringly and ran her hand affectionately through my hair. "What's the matter, son? Don't you feel well? You look haggard."

"I feel all right," I said.

I escaped her and sat alone on the back porch until called to the table. When supper was safely over my situation was unimproved. It was too late to go outside again, and I could not long remain in the house without meeting my father. At the latest it could be put off only till family prayer. Perhaps that was the time when my crime would be related. Maybe they would pray for me and then expel me from home. I had just begun drying the dishes when the long-awaited sound was heard.

"Son."

It was not the wrathful voice I had expected. It was calm, just loud enough to be audible. Nevertheless it was enough to make me tremble and drop a spoon. For a moment it seemed I could not move.

"Your daddy wants you, dear."

I put down the dishtowel and went to the door of the porch.

"Yes, sir."

"Come out here where I can see you."

"I approached the bed. My hands were clenched and I was biting my lip, trying not to cry.

"Your mother tells me you haven't been eating well today. You aren't sick, are you?"

"No, sir."

"You feel all right?"

"Yes, sir."

"Sit down, son. I just called you out here to talk for a while. I often think we don't talk to each other enough. I guess that's my fault. We'll have to do better in the future. I'd like to hear more about what you're interested in and what you think, because that's the only way I can get to know you." He paused a moment. "Maybe you think because I'm grown up I understand everything, but that's not true. You'll find as you get older that no matter how much you learn there's always much you don't know. For example, you're my own son and I ought to know you pretty well, but every now and then something'll happen that'll make me realize I don't understand you at all."

I choked back a sob and tried to brace myself for the coming blow.

"I don't think I ever understood my own father," he went on presently, "until it was too late. We were very poor—much poorer, son, than you can imagine. From year in to year out we might see only a few dollars in our house, and what little there was had to be saved for essentials. When we sold our cotton we'd have to buy a plow or an ax. And there were staple foods we had to buy like flour and sugar. We bought cloth, too, but never any ready-made clothes. Until I was a grown man I never had any clothes except what my mother made. I got my first store-bought suit to go away to medical school in, and I don't believe my mother ever had a store-bought dress. My father worked hard and made his boys work hard. We resented it and sometimes even hated him for it, but in the end we knew he was right. One of my brothers never could get along with Daddy, and he ran away from home when he was fifteen. He turned out to be a no-account scoundrel, and the last I heard of him he was a saloon keeper in New Orleans.

"In the summer we hoed corn and picked cotton, and in the winter we fixed rail fences and chopped wood and hauled it home. And always there were mules and pigs to take care of. It was a very different life from yours . . . and in some ways a better one." He looked at me affectionately. "At any rate, we learned how to work, and there's nothing more

important for a boy to learn. It's something you
haven't yet learned, son. Isn't that right?"

"Yes, sir."

"You will, though. If you ever amount to anything
you'll learn. You're learning now. I wish you could
understand, though, that I wouldn't be trying to
teach you so fast if I knew I would live long enough
to teach you more slowly." He paused a moment.
"Do you have anything to say?"

"No, sir."

"Then I guess you'd better see if your mother
needs you."

I stood up, hardly able to believe that this was all.

"Son."

"Yes, sir."

"Come here a minute."

I went to the bed and my father put a hand on
my shoulder. "Remember, son," he said in a husky
voice, "whenever it seems I'm being hard on you . . .
it's because I love you."

Late that night I woke in terror from a nightmare.
For several minutes I lay in bed trembling, unable
to convince myself that it was just a dream. Presently
I got up and tiptoed through the dark house to the
porch.

"Daddy?" I whispered. "Daddy . . . are you all
right?"

There was no reply, but soon I became aware of
his regular breathing. I went back to bed but almost
immediately got up and knelt on the floor. "Dear
God, please don't let anything happen to Daddy.
Amen."

Still I could not sleep. I lay in bed and thought of
many things and after a while began worrying about
the razor. What had I done with it? Was it still on

the ground under the awning? Perhaps I had left it open. Someone might step on it and get cut. I got up again and went outside looking for it. In the dark I felt about on the ground under my father's windows but did not find it. Then I went to the barn and found it in its usual place, properly closed.

The next morning before noon I finished the job. The last blade of grass was cut and carried away and the back yard was as bald as a razor could make it.

"Daddy," I said, standing under the porch windows, "I've finished. Is it all right?"

He looked over the yard, then took his binoculars and scrutinized it in more detail, particularly the corners.

"That's well done, son."

I put away the basket and razor and came inside. After dinner I began to feel uncomfortable. It seemed strange not to be working. Restless, unable to sit still, I wandered about the house, looking out the windows and wondering what to do. Presently I sought and obtained permission to go to Paul's house, but somehow felt I was doing something wrong.

During the next two weeks I often played with my friends but never fully lost myself in play and was secretly glad when school started and life settled down to a routine again. I was more quiet than before and better behaved, and when next the report cards were distributed I had a nearly perfect score in conduct.

HEROES

I remember being at a point below his knees and looking up at the vast length of him. He was six foot three; his voice was big. He was devastatingly attractive—even to his daughter as a child. . . . His voice was so beautiful, so enveloping. He was just bigger and better than anyone else.

ANJELICA HUSTON

Papa was a man of brimstone and hot fire, in his mind and in his fists, and was known . . . as the champion of all the fist fighters. He used his fists on sharks and fakers, and all to give his family nice things. WOODY GUTHRIE

I always kind of figured he was more of a social activist than a political activist. He invented his own social structure that he wanted to see happen, so every time he was aware of an injustice, he would

invent a right [to counter it]. That was his basic political platform. I think that's what I like about him:
that individual liberty not to go along with any
group, but to think of what's right or wrong on your
own.

ARLO GUTHRIE of his father, Woody Guthrie

My father moved through our town like a white god
in a native village. He was a manager for the Southern Coal and Coke Company and totally beloved and
respected by all his friends and all who worked for
him. At harvest time the local farmers could not wait
to give him their first melons and corn. They would
never allow other hunters on their land, but gave
him permission to enter their sanctuary for quail or
pigeon as if his gun did not kill. His physical dimen-
sions can only be described as—shall I say it?—fat!
He was a great fat man. But it was absolutely right.
His body complemented an immense spirit that
seemed to wrap itself around everyone. When I am
asked why I wanted to be an actress, I always say,
"I don't really know, I just did." But I think I
wanted to have everybody love me, the way they
loved Daddy. PATRICIA NEAL

One of Yul's more memorable demonstrations of
self-sufficiency occurred one idyllic morning when
he'd come home from the theater with Don, and
we'd gone straight on to the boat to ski on the [Long
Island] Sound. We had come a long way out from
port, to be clear of traffic. Dad was in the water, and
Don tossed him the tow-handle; it struck his head,
putting a two-inch gash in that famous pate.

Dad was disgusted that our day had been ruined. It wasn't a serious wound, even though it bled profusely; still, we would have to cruise into Westport to find a doctor or an emergency room. Unless ... In our toolkit Yul found a set of small fishing hooks, and thin nylon line. As Don held the mirror and I watched, Yul used one hook to thread two stitches through the flaps of bleeding flesh and tie them shut. A half hour later he was skiing again.

ROCK BRYNNER of his father, Yul Brynner

In 1909, when he was twenty-one years old, my father walked into a second-floor dentist's office opposite City Hall. He sat down in the chair and pointed to his crooked teeth. "Pull them out," he said.

"All of them?" the dentist said.

"All of them," my father said.

It took about four hours and cost $200. My father had to go to bed for the rest of the day, the pain was so acute. He spent another $250 for a set of good false teeth. Within a week he looked in the mirror and saw a handsome man.

Whenever I walked past City Hall in Jersey City and looked across the street at the site of the dentist's office, which was long gone, my mouth hurt. I felt my father's pain. I admired his guts. I wondered if I could do something so daring. My father had done nothing less than change himself from an ugly lower-class Irish-American—a mick—to a man with good looks that belonged to no particular group. The price he paid in pain and money was unquestionably worth it.   THOMAS FLEMING

My father was a big drinker, spent most of his time in saloons, much of it in fights. Once he got into a brawl with seven men. He tossed one through a window, jumped over the bar, and brained a few more with bottles. Laid them all out. In court, the judge looked at the crowd accusing my father of giving them black eyes, broken noses, bruised ribs, and threw the case out: he didn't believe that one man could beat up so many people. There were other stories about my father that raised him to the level of legend: that he popped metal bottle caps and crushed shot glasses with his teeth; that he would go from saloon to saloon with an iron bar, betting for drinks that he could bend it with his bare hands, and doing it; that nobody could beat him at arm wrestling. He was probably the toughest, strongest Jew in our town, the *bulvan*. There were other Jewish peddlers, but none of them dared to go up on Cork Hill, the Irish section. Pa did. Ma warned me not to be like him.   KIRK DOUGLAS

My dad certainly was no sissy, little guy that he was. The janitor of our apartment house was a big, ugly brute. His fourteen-year-old son was cast in his image. One day, as I turned into the walkway leading to the front of our building, Sonny Boy grabbed me and began pounding on me. No reason. He simply had nothing else to do at that moment.

When my dad found out, he went right downstairs to brace the janitor. Ignatz (or whatever his name was) stood out front, watering the sparse little lawn in front of the place. I watched out the window as my brave little dad shook a finger in the face of the big oaf, shouting at him and warning him to tell his kid to lay off me.

"Ignatz" took it for a while. Then he casually turned and slammed my dad in the face. Blood spurted from Dad's nose and down he went, tripping over the little wire fence that separated the sidewalk from the grass. Dad got up. The bastard knocked him down again. It was David and Goliath, except this time, William David Tormé was getting the worst of it. The janitor looked down at my dad, spit on the lawn, and walked unconcernedly away. Dad came back upstairs, holding a handkerchief to his nose. His eyes were tearing in humiliation. He walked into his bedroom and closed the door. I never felt so impotent in my life.

The next day, my beloved uncle Al put his two cents in. Al, my musical mentor, Al of the sweet disposition, Al who became a major in World War II and saw active duty in the Pacific. Al, with delightful simplicity, walked up to "Ignatz" during the latter's daily grass-watering session and, without a word, decked him. And decked him again. And again. The bum went to the hospital. Al explained to the police, summoned by the janitor's wife, what had happened. When they took a look at my dad, they actually grinned at my uncle and drove away.   MEL TORMÉ

It took place back in Grand Island [Nebraska] when I was five. My father, uncle and grandfather Cavett were bowling, and I and my four-year-old cousin were wandering around. My cousin somehow irritated one of the other bowlers, who picked him up and dumped him heavily on a bench. My cousin screamed bloody murder. My father turned, saw my cousin pointing at this guy, and started toward him with a murderous look in his eye. The guy headed for the door, thereby sealing his fate. Whatever my father imagined had taken place filled him with righteous wrath, and he took off in pursuit, followed by the entire population of the bowling alley. The culprit was larger than my father, which probably explains why my father caught up with him about half a block away, both of them out of breath. My father sent him rolling on the sidewalk with a well-placed knee to the small of the back. The guy got up and ran another half block to a diner and tore inside, apparently thinking that not even an enraged English teacher would continue a fight in a crowded diner. My uncle had been carrying me under one arm and my cousin under the other, but somehow I got loose and tore ahead to where the action was. I got inside the diner in time to see my father unleash a well-aimed right to the jaw that sent the guy about five feet backward into a stack of pop-bottle cases. Cases and bottles came crashing down around him in a spectacular cascade that was as good as anything I had seen in the movies. Just then the guy's wife, who had apparently decided somebody ought to salvage the family honor, grabbed my father's arm and ripped his shirt sleeve off. Being a gentleman, he ignored the crowd's exhortations to flatten her too and decided it was time to depart.

Later, when two cops arrived at our house to investigate the incident, they turned out to be former high school classmates of my father's. Thanks to them, the newspaper account made it appear that my grandfather had done the fighting. Even though this undoubtedly protected my father's job, I felt cheated. I

guess I wanted to see a headline saying DICK CA-
VETT'S FATHER PULVERIZES BULLY.   DICK CAVETT

Though he never went into the army (excused from
service because he had too many children), he would
have made a good soldier. He was intelligent and
stoic and did not shirk duty. I am not romanticizing,
I hope, when I say that he would have run into a
burning building to pull us out, without giving any
thought to his safety. I still get shivers remembering
one occasion when he risked his neck. We were
locked out of our house—someone had lost the keys
during a family outing—and my father went next
door to see if he could leap from the neighbor's fire
escape to ours. It was no small distance; if he slipped
and fell he would hit solid cement. We couldn't see
how he was doing because the fire escapes were all
on the back side of the building and we waited in
the front vestibule. My brother Hal started whistling
the Funeral March. "Hope you like being a widow.
Was that a splat?" he said, cocking his ear. Ordinarily, sarcasm and gallows humor were the preferred family style, but this time my mother chewed
her lips and stared through the locked glass door,
holding her mouton coat closed at the throat. She
had tried to talk my father out of the attempt, insisting they could call the police to break down the
door, but my father wouldn't hear of it. This was his
job. I remember my mother's terrified, tear-streaked
face while she waited in suspense. Molly said, "Ma, I
don't think this is such a good idea," and my mother
slapped her across the face for saying what all of us
were thinking. Eventually we saw my father's trou-
sers coming downstairs, the whole of him shortly
after. When he let us in, we kids cheered: "Our

hero!" "Don't give me that bullshit," said my father, modestly and gruffly.　　　　　PHILLIP LOPATE

My father was two men, one sympathetic and intuitional, the other critical and logical; altogether they formed a combination that could not be thrown off its feet.　　　JULIAN HAWTHORNE of his father, Nathaniel Hawthorne

When he decided that he was addicted to drugs and that that was bad, he committed himself. This was at a very late stage in his life. He must have been very close to seventy. That's very hard, physically. No one made that decision for him or talked him into it. It was strictly on his own. He was subjected to horrible treatment, because that kind of thing wasn't in vogue when he did it. I think he was very brave.

　　　　　　　　　　　　BELA LUGOSI, JR.

One time, when I was young, we were at a restaurant, and we had a little black girl with us, Jeannie, who was a cousin of the woman who took care of me. And this drunk came over. Now, drunks have always scared me, and they still scare me, because whenever I saw a drunk it would be a big guy and wobbling and not knowing what he's going to do. He said something, and Dad was trying to be nice, and then he said something about the little black girl and sort of touched Mom. Dad jumped up and smashed him in the face, and the guy went sailing. Literally, one hit, knocked him out. And I applauded.

JOHN RITTER of his father, Tex Ritter

The University of Berlin, 1934, ten years before my birth. He has come from Pennsylvania, the son of Russian immigrants, to do graduate work in German literature. Registration takes place in a large hall, filled with students.

He gets to the head of his line, a small American flag pinned to his lapel, and the Registrar asks him a question, in German, which he has not asked anyone preceding him.

"What percentage non-Aryan are you?"

"One hundred percent American," he says, his face flushed. The man asks again, raising his voice. "What percentage non-Aryan are you?"

The huge room suddenly goes silent, focusing on them. He leans forward, pounds his fist onto the table, and shouts in the man's face, "One hundred percent non-Aryan. One hundred percent American!"

The whole room bursts into applause. He is twenty-four.   DAVID EPSTEIN

I can remember trying to confront the source of the family's unspoken troubles only once with my father, after he had been hauled before the Eastland committee in the Senate—I'm not exactly sure how long after, maybe a few weeks, maybe it was even months. We were riding in the car, just the two of us in the family's beat-up '47 Plymouth, and I came right out and asked the question, with even fewer formalities than the Senator had seen fit to observe. "Dad, are you a Communist?" Just like that.

More than anything, I remember the silence that followed and my not daring to look at him, staring instead at the green metal dash, waiting, hoping. I suppose the silence told me more than the answer that finally followed, was more definitive, but I was hardly listening anyway by that time: I was aware at last how much my question had hurt him. I had no sense then, of course, that the child's question was far tougher than the Senator's. In answering Eastland he could at least maintain some semblance of dignity, honor, principle. My question offered no escape; there is no Fifth Amendment for eight-year-olds. Surely he knew this. The answer I wanted was no, and I like to think now that he tried to give it to me. The temptation to lie must have been great, but it was too late and he knew it. There was nothing left to do but dissemble. Yes, he had been accused of being a Communist, by a man who had no real way of knowing whether he was a Democrat, a Republican, or a Communist. The man was a well-known liar and these were bad times—charges were flying everywhere, outrageous charges, unfair charges. Many friends of the family had also been accused, and there was no truth to most of what people were saying or what the newspapers were reporting. The fact was that he and Mom and their friends were *progressive* people who were being smeared because of what they believed in—not because they were members of the Communist party.

I didn't ask any questions when he finished explaining, and I'm sure he guessed that my silence meant that I knew. It took twenty-five years before I asked him that question again. When we got home and out of the car on that afternoon in 1952, he put his arm around me and held me close to him as we walked toward the house. At that moment, perhaps for the first time, I felt protective toward him.

CARL BERNSTEIN

My father used to say there are two kinds of people: those who stop at an accident and those who drive by. He was the kind who would help.

MARLO THOMAS

My father, as a diplomat, could not express any feelings about what was wrong. However, at one point a southern senator wrote him a letter saying it had been noticed that a lot of black people came to the embassy and entered through the front door, and that in the United States they used the service entrance. And my father said that he came from a very religious family which had always kept up a halfway house [for the poor and hungry]—which I still keep up today. He said, "In our house, everybody can come through the front door." AHMET ERTEGUN

One Sunday, the minister began to preach a sermon on infants in hell—fire, brimstone, the works—who had somehow fallen under the power of the devil. Father, who was a regular churchgoer, became very angry at the preacher. We were all together for a family gathering, and when the preacher started to describe the awful fate of these doomed babies, my father rose from his seat, pointed to the preacher, and said, "Sir, you are a liar." He got all his family out of the pew, and ushered us into the street.

MARTHA GRAHAM

There was quite a lot of racism going on because we were the only black family for miles [in the Hancock Park section of Los Angeles]. Before I was born, one of the women there approached my father and told him, "Well, you know, we don't want any *undesirables* in this neighborhood." And my father just looked at her and said, "Well, if I see any I'll let you know." Another time when we lived there, this real socialite lady who lived down the street in, literally, a glass house was having a luncheon. She invited my dad, and when he got there they wanted him to perform. So being the gracious man that he was, he did. But he also sent her a bill for his services. So my dad was cool, you know. He was hip to people. People tend to think he was just a nice wimp. But he was a strong, religious man who knew what was going on.

NATALIE COLE, of her father, Nat "King" Cole

I can always count on thinking of my father at the same time each day: when I shave. He recommended a new shaving cream to me before he died, and he turned out to be right.

We had a chance to get closer before he died. He seemed pleased with what I'd accomplished in life. My father was a very reasonable man. Cerebral. A teacher. Sentimental. Outwardly jovial much of the time, in a way that concealed a basic Baptist puritanism. Let's just say he wasn't overconfident. Or materialistic. [*Ponders a while*] He was married once.

WARREN BEATTY

My father was very strong. I don't agree with a lot of the ways he brought me up. I don't agree with a lot of his values, but he did have a lot of integrity, and if he told us not to do something, he didn't do it, either. A lot of parents tell their kids not to smoke cigarettes and they smoke cigarettes. Or they give you some idea of sexual modesty—but my father lived that way. He believed that making love to someone is a very sacred thing and it shouldn't happen until after you are married. He stuck by those beliefs, and that represented a very strong person to me. He was my role model. MADONNA

My mother always deferred to my father, and in his absence spoke of him to me as if he were all-wise. I confused him in some sense with God; at all events I believed that my father knew everything and saw everything. One morning in my sixth year, my mother and I were alone in the morning room, when my father came in and announced some fact to us. I was standing on the rug, gazing at him, and when he made this statement, I remember turning quickly, in embarrassment, and looking into the fire. The shock to me was as that of a thunderbolt, for what my father had said was not true. My mother and I, who had been present at the trifling incident, were aware that it had not happened precisely as it had been reported to him. My mother gently told him so, and he accepted the correction. Nothing could possibly have been more trifling to my parents, but to me it meant an epoch. Here was the appalling discovery, never suspected before, that my father was not as God, and did not know everything. EDMUND GOSSE

People were always drawn to Papa—men, women, children—even animals. The one thing that he didn't attract was money. He was one of those individuals who, in spite of his intelligence and ambition, worked hard all his life without ever achieving financial success. He started working as a child and, except for a few brief holidays now and again, never stopped working until he was in his late sixties.

He had jobs in noisy factories, greasy kitchens, crowded hotels, and frenzied restaurants. Though he was a consistently valued employee, he was always somehow passed over at promotion time. Twice he started his own businesses and both times the partners whom he trusted found means of easing him out or absconding with the profits, leaving him with the accumulated debts.

Papa was forever considered too generous. It was a common thing to hear people say of him, "He's too good. He's not aggressive enough. He's too meek, and in America the meek don't inherit much of anything, let alone the earth."

I remember some difficult times when I was growing up, times when we questioned whether we'd have enough food to eat or be able to meet the monthly bills. But I never recall having been hungry, and never at any time did it occur to me that Papa might be a failure.   LEO BUSCAGLIA

He loved challenges of all kinds—especially those which engaged the mind. . . . I remember when he received the Legion d'honneur—a tribute he was tremendously proud of. . . . He chose to give his acceptance speech at the French consulate in French, in which he was a little bit rusty. What made it a particular challenge was that in his speech he told a funny story. That is truly a challenge—to tell a funny story in rusty French to a room full of French dignitaries. I will tell you the story but not in French. I did not learn that much courage from my father. It was a story about the difficulty of communication—a United Nations kind of story. Father described how he had gone to a movie theater off the Champs-Elysees where an American Western was being shown in English with the subtitles in French. At one point a gunslinger, a very rough sort, had shot up a bar, his guns blazing, and afterward had swaggered up to the bar, where he said, "Gimme a shot of red-eye!" The subtitle to translate this read as follows: *"Donnez-moi un Dubonnet, s'il vous plait."*

GEORGE PLIMPTON

Aissa Wayne

from

John Wayne, My Father

On Monday, April 9, I did not accompany him to the Academy Awards. There was a shortage of tickets that year for presenters, and my father had promised Marisa, who'd only been three when he won for *True Grit*, that one day he'd take her with him to the Oscars. Perhaps he believed this would be his last chance.

The afternoon of the show I stopped in at my father's suite at the Bonaventure Hotel, a short drive from the Music Center in downtown Los Angeles, the venue for that night's telecast. To appear less emaciated, by then he'd begun wearing loose-fitting clothes around the house and extra layers of clothing the few times he went out in public. For the Oscars, he had ordered a smaller tuxedo, but kept losing weight in the interim. That afternoon, his new tux already too large, he put on a wet suit beneath it to make himself look heavier.

Along with his weight, he felt anxious about the best picture award he'd been chosen to present. He did not want to mangle names, which even at his best my father was prone to do. He was most concerned about Warren Beatty, the producer-star of *Heaven Can Wait*. Warren Beatty, my father said, hated it when people called him Warren *Beety*. Determined to say it correctly, my father practiced again and again in the mirror: "Warren *Beatty*. Warren *Beatty*. Warren *Beatty*."

Late that afternoon I drove back to Newport alone to make it home in time for the show, but a part of me was hoping my dad would decide on a last-minute cancellation. For all I knew this night meant to him, when I left him he looked peaked. For several weeks he'd had trouble merely standing for any extended duration, and now he was sick and the Oscars was such a long show and best picture award always came at the very end. I was scared he might be exhausted by then, walk out, and collapse on national TV. Even if he recovered, I knew what that would do to my father's pride.

My father, of course, showed up, and by then I had changed my mind. He'd been so dead set on making this engagement, to miss it now could debilitate him even more than sticking it out could. That evening I watched the awards on TV with a handful of friends, and the show ran long as usual. Finally, the producers ran a clip of Bob Hope, pulled from the Oscar one year before, when my father was bedridden at Massachusetts General.

"Duke, we miss you tonight," Bob Hope said. "We expect to see you amble out here in person next year, because nobody else can walk in John Wayne's boots."

From the image of Mr. Hope, the camera swung back to Johnny Carson, this evening's emcee. "Ladies, Gentlemen," Johnny Carson said, "Mr. John Wayne."

By the time my father reached the Music Center stage, the industry crowd rose as one and its standing ovation swelled to a human crescendo. They clapped so heartfelt and long—for the voice, the walk, the classic lines and scenes, his bravery and his will—my father could not start his speech. Watching at home I barely breathed. Pride welled in my throat, and my heart said, *Keep on clapping forever, let it wash over him, he needs your love, it will give him strength.* But my rational mind said, *Stop, he can't stand up, stop and let him get off, can't you see he's not going to make it?*

The camera panned the seats as the Hollywood people cried. My own tears came as they zoomed back in for another close-up. He was perspiring now, and he looked so deathly thin. It was like watching him walk a tightrope.

When the clapping finally died, my father spoke in a shaking voice: "That's just about the only medicine a fella'd ever really need. Believe me when I tell you that I'm mighty pleased that I can amble down here tonight. Oscar and I have something in common. Oscar came to the Hollywood scene in 1928—so did I. We're both a little weatherbeaten, but we're still here, and plan to be around a whole lot longer. My job here tonight is to identify your five choices for the outstanding picture of the year and announce the winner, so let's move 'em out."

My father kept on, announcing the nominees, and then he came to Warren Beatty. And my father could not say it right. Still, even then, John Wayne got it wrong uniquely: he didn't stumble on Beatty, but my father called him "Warner." I let out a nervous laugh and one of my girlfriends said, "What?"

I was so absorbed in my father I'd forgotten I wasn't alone.

The Deer Hunter won best picture, and when my dad presented the Oscar to its director, Michael Cimino, he called him Michael "Camino." I cried and laughed then, too, but when it was over a few mispronounced names meant nothing at all, except perhaps to my stubborn dad. For the rest of us watching that indelible night, I think we all felt honored and moved, and that we had all shared in something resoundingly special. It was his final appearance in public, John Wayne's last public battle. I won't say he won—he was still dying of cancer— but, oh, what a fight my courageous father put up.

Arthur Ashe

Seasoned Wood

My father was the caretaker for the largest playground for blacks in Richmond, Virginia. He assumed that position in 1948, when segregation was still very much in place in Virginia.

He was a man who set a very strong example. I got to see him day in and day out live the advice he gave me. He thought men should be at home when they didn't have anything in particular to do. My father has never been to a bar, he didn't drink, much, hardly at all. I've never seen my father even tipsy, let alone drunk. He smoked for a while and then stopped. Had a very sharply demarcated sense of right and wrong, grounded of course in southern rural biblical bromides. He put great store in education, something he didn't have but he thought would serve his children and everybody else's children well. He was not at all fooled by the discrepancy between what society pretended was equal opportunity and what reality was. He wasn't fooled by the Pledge of Allegiance; he knew it didn't apply to blacks.

I did very, very well in school, I was a bright kid,

I guess, and my father was, in absolute terms, unlettered. So early on I felt a great division between our two ways of thinking, but it didn't diminish my respect for him.

When I was a boy they started to build Interstate 95, which now goes from Maine to Florida. When they were building I-95 through Richmond, it went right through some black neighborhoods, literally within a block of my school, Baker Elementary. At that time my father decided he didn't really want to live in Richmond permanently, so, working in his spare time and on weekends, with the help of my brother and myself, my father collected the raw materials from the bulldozed structures making way for I-95 and built his own house in Gumspring, Virginia, twenty-eight miles away.

That's where my stepmother lives even now, in the house that my father built with his very own hands. He was very industrious. He attended the old CCC, Civilian Conservation Corps, camps, where he learned some other skills in addition to those you would ordinarily learn if you are very self-sufficient. But I guess the house topped it all off. We collected the bricks and cinder blocks from old torn-down public housing units—perfectly good cinder blocks that were just going to be crushed and made into road gravel or something—perfectly good bricks and wood. I remember my father exclaiming, "Seasoned wood!"

That experience has materially influenced my ideas about what to do about a lot of social ills, ideas which often put me at counterpoint to professional sociologists. I have a very low exasperation level for people who use the lack of education or opportunity as an excuse to do nothing because I saw my father, functionally illiterate, in a racist situation, make a success of himself.

CHARACTERS

My father was a conservative Republican. When the *New Yorker* published a profile of Franklin Delano Roosevelt, he cancelled our subscription.

JULIA CHILD

My father was very prejudiced; he never lived to see his dream of an all Yiddish-speaking Canada.

DAVID STEINBERG

For my father, the refusal of anyone in the twentieth century to become part of the Catholic church was not pitiable; it was malicious and willful. Culpable ignorance, he called it. He loved the sense of his own orthodoxy, of holding out for the purest and the finest and the most refined sense of truth against the slick hucksters who promised happiness on earth and the supremacy of human reason.

In history, his sympathies were with the Royalists

71

in the French Revolution, the South in the Civil War, the Russian czar, the Spanish Fascists. He believed that Voltaire and Rousseau could be held (and that God was at this very moment holding them) personally responsible for the mess of the twentieth century.   MARY GORDON, from *Final Payments*

My father hated radio and could not wait for television to be invented so he could hate that too.

PETER DE VRIES

My father hated France. He said that he hated it because most of his army infantry platoon was slaughtered on the beach at Normandy—by a lucky chance he was transferred out of the platoon and north to a cushy job with the Signal Corps in Astoria, Queens, just before they shipped out—but I think he avoided France because of my mother's infatuation with the country, and because she spoke the language and he didn't.   SUSAN CHEEVER

I once said to my father when I was a boy, "Dad, we need a third political party." He said, "I'll settle for a second."   RALPH NADER

In Africa, when the sun goes down, the stars spring up, all of them in their expected places, glittering and moving. In the rainy season, the sky flashed and thundered. In the dry season, the great dark hollow of night was lit by veld fires: the mountains burned through September and October in chains of red fire. Every night my father took out his chair to watch the sky and the mountains, smoking, silent, a thin shabby fly-away figure under the stars. "Makes you think—there are so many worlds up there, wouldn't really matter if we did blow ourselves up— plenty more where we came from." DORIS LESSING

[My father's] manners were always courteous, he was kind. He had very beautiful large hands, and the only lack of refinement I remember in him was an unconscious habit he had, while reading his newspaper in his armchair, of picking his nose abstractedly and rolling the little bit of snot between his thumb and forefinger.   J. R. ACKERLEY

My father, like most Englishmen, could commit assault and battery with politeness.   FLORENCE KING

He had the precious gift of being deaf when convenient. Many people took this for absent-mindedness, but it was rather his faculty for concentrating on what suited him, and remaining impervious to what seemed inappropriate or useless. He was in no way a daydreamer: or at any rate his dreams were based on a sharp observation of life, for in order to grasp reality better he limited his perceptions to a few definite things.   JEAN RENOIR

[My father] had a rapier-like wit at the expense of the absent. Nobody left the dining room until after he did—and not out of respect.

JACK L. WARNER, JR.

I was always terrified of what my father was going to say to the press. When they asked him what he thought of the permissive society he said he wished to God it had been invented sixty years ago!

EDWARD HEATH

My father used to say,
"Superior people never make long visits,
have to be shown Longfellow's grave
or the glass flowers at Harvard."

MARIANNE MOORE

Father was a perfectionist. We had to hop to everything and have marvelous table manners. I could only wear navy blue and gray and white. He wanted me to be interested in tennis and horses just like a little princess, but I couldn't stand such things.

RAQUEL WELCH

My father thought of Russia as a land of cornfields and happy laughter, and he used to drop copies of the *Daily Worker* around casually for people to read. Mother was always hissing at him and telling him to pick them up.

DAVID HOCKNEY

After the bath it was time to clean the vocal apparatus. He turned on the inhalator, a small boiler with an alcohol burner. The boiler was filled with water, and its atomizer at the end of a tube led into a container filled with a glycerine solution. He would cover his head with a towel and lean over the equipment. When the atomizer began to spurt steam, it created a fine spray. He inhaled deeply, his mouth wide open. The nicotine deposits in his throat and bronchial tubes made his sputum come up in great globs of black phlegm at first. Then with each cough it lightened, until in fifteen or twenty minutes he would bring up nothing but clear white saliva. Satisfied, he would turn off the inhalator.

"*Lo strumento e pulito*"—"The instrument is clean," he would declare.

And he would reach for a cigarette and light up.
ENRICO CARUSO, JR.

My mother said he was proud of me and I suppose he was. But he was very Germanic and didn't like to show emotions. The first decent season I had I conducted the Philharmonic in New York and at Cleveland, Philadelphia and Minneapolis. When I told him, all he said was, "So they didn't want you at Boston, then?"
ANDRÉ PREVIN

My father refused to have his photograph taken because he, like the Indians, believed that the camera captured your spirit.
ALICE KAHN

One time Dr. Kully asked Pop why he did not go back to writing for the movie studios, "just to make some money for the family." (Many were under the impression that Pop was not too well off financially because he was not a natty dresser, and he drove an inexpensive, five-year-old car.) "Can't you just knock off one or two scripts to make expenses?" Barney said.

Pop sighed, then said, "Barney, would you like to go through the rest of your medical career circumsizing rabbits?"

WILL FOWLER of his father, Gene Fowler

As a boy, I had a cat named Mackenzie who was particularly adamant in his opposition to pills. I can remember one terribly worrisome night when my father and I tried to administer medication to him. I don't know how I succeeded in involving my father in the project. He didn't like cats and, when we had them, always insisted on not knowing their names. He addressed them and referred to them by their colors: "Hello, brown cat," or "I saw the gray-and-white cat devouring a toad near the driveway."

COLIN McENROE

My father ... loved to stand in front of a theater where a play of mine was on and every once in a while stroll in to chat with the box office men about business. "How do you know they're giving you the right count?" he would ask me. Indeed, how did I?

In 1962, after our divorce, Marilyn took him as

her escort to John Kennedy's birthday party in Madison Square Garden and introduced him to the president. My father would treasure a news photographer's picture of the occasion: Marilyn stands laughing with her head thrown back while Kennedy shakes hands with him, laughing with spontaneous, innocent enjoyment at what I am sure must have been one of my father's surprising remarks. I was not aware that for the rest of his life, which lasted some four more years, he spent considerable time on the lookout for his name in the gossip columns and entertainment news, until one day he gravely asked me—he was about eighty then—"Do you look like me or do I look like you?"

This was serious. "I guess I look like you," I said. He seemed to like that answer.　　ARTHUR MILLER

My father always wanted to be the corpse at every funeral, the bride at every wedding and the baby at every christening.
　　　　　ALICE ROOSEVELT LONGWORTH,
　　　　　of her father, Theodore Roosevelt

My dad's idea of a good time is to go to Sears and walk around.　　　　　　　　　　　JAY LENO

We had a very nice house and my dad had a whole collection of Nazi war relics: daggers, guns, machine guns, uniforms, banners. Growing up and seeing those items, I actually thought the Nazis won the war, and I thought we were the Nazis.
　　THOR SADLER,
　　son of Green Beret Staff Sergeant Barry Sadler

Often our father overawed us, not by any harshness, but by his nocturnal quality. He was at home in the night, and made it more mysterious. I remember when I was about six waking up with the darkness thick about me, and calling to my mother and getting no answer, and crawling to her bed and finding it empty. I came to the conclusion that war had broken out, some war that had escaped out of a book. I accepted that I must fight, and got down on the carpet and crawled toward the thin yellow line that marked the opening of the door, just ajar.

When I pushed it open I saw three people outside my sister Winifred's bedroom on the other side of the landing in a disordered group: my mother in her dressing-gown, her hair wild about her shoulders, our doctor in an overcoat over his pyjamas, with a stethoscope waving in one hand like a strand of creeper, and my father, dressed as he would have been in the daytime, in clothes that had a curiously Wild West look, but very neat, and self-possessed as he would have been if he had been greeting a visitor he knew but not very well. I was not at all alarmed by my mother and the doctor, who looked exactly as I expected people would who were pulled so far out of the ordinary routine as to be walking about in the middle of the night. But I was horror-stricken because my father seemed completely unaffected by the fact that that was exactly what it was: the middle of the night. He was talking clearly and persuasively, making explanatory gestures when he ought to be in bed. I shuddered, seeing him as unabashed by a law which I had, indeed, every reason to consider as sacred as any law, since it was so universally obeyed. REBECCA WEST

Daddy had got us rooms in a motel until he could find us a house. There were not a lot of places available for a young family on our budget. Daddy went around to dozens of places. Nobody wanted kids. Finally, he found one in the hills south of Glendale. As usual, the landlady asked if he had kids.

"Yep," he replied, "boy and a girl. Ages seven and nine."

"Well, whatta you going to do about them?" she wanted to know, implying that she didn't allow children.

"I'm gonna take 'em out and drown 'em in the Los Angeles River tonight and come back tomorrow." That was my father—ask a silly question and just wait. She must have had the same sense of humor: We moved in the next day.

DEBBIE REYNOLDS

"I brought you into this world," my father would say, "and I can take you out. It don't make no difference to me. I'll just make another one like you."

BILL COSBY

Arthur Marx

from

Life With Groucho

My father hated sight-seeing . . . but once when we were on a trip to Salt Lake City with him, Mother talked him into going on a guided tour through the Mormon Tabernacle. My father's deportment was admirable through most of the proceedings, and he even seemed to be interested when the guide stopped the group in the main auditorium and started to lecture us about the fine acoustics in the building.

This is the high point of the tour through the Tabernacle, and the guide always finishes his talk by announcing that the acoustics are so amazing that you can "actually hear a pin drop. To prove it, ladies and gentlemen, I'm going to drop a pin, and I want you to be very quiet and listen to it drop."

A rapt silence settled over the group as the guide took a pin from his coat pocket, held it in the air dramatically for a moment, and then let it fall to the floor. You couldn't hear the pin drop, but the people, obviously mesmerized by the ritual, imagined that they did, and nodded their approval.

"I see you all heard it," said the pleased guide, ready to move on to another point of interest.

"I couldn't hear a thing," answered Groucho in a loud tone from the rear of the group. "Would you mind dropping it again? And use a bigger pin this time—a bowling pin. I'm a little hard of hearing!"

A burly guide approached him from the rear and tapped him on the shoulder. "We don't want any wiseguys around here, mister. We'd like you to leave now, without giving us any trouble."

"I'm not a wiseguy. But I paid my money, and I think I'm entitled to hear a pin drop."

"Would you like us to call the police?"

"You can't arrest me. Don't you know who I am?"

My father was aroused, and my mother, though annoyed, was at least pleased that he was going to abandon his mantle of anonymity to save us from complete disgrace.

"No, who are you?" asked the guide. He still didn't know my father, but there must have been a spark of recognition, for his tone had softened somewhat.

"My name's Jackson," said my father. "Sam Jackson. And this is Mrs. Jackson, of the Stonewall Jacksons."

The Jacksons were promptly expelled from the Mormon Tabernacle, and my mother and father didn't speak for the remainder of the trip.

C. S. Lewis

from

Surprised by Joy

It was axiomatic to my father (in theory) that nothing was said or done from an obvious motive. Hence he who in his real life was the most honorable and impulsive of men, and the easiest victim that any knave or imposter could hope to meet, became a positive Machiavel when he knitted his brows and applied to the behavior of people he had never seen the spectral and labyrinthine operation which he called "reading between the lines." Once embarked upon that, he might make his landfall anywhere in the wide world: and always with unshakable conviction. "I see it all"—"I understand it perfectly"—"It's as plain as a pikestaff," he would say; and then, as we soon learned, he would believe till his dying day in some deadly quarrel, some slight, some secret sorrow or some immensely complex machination, which was not only improbable but impossible. Dissent on our part was attributed with kindly laughter, to our innocence, gullibility, and general ignorance of life. And besides all these confusions, there were the

sheer *non sequiturs* when the ground seemed to open
at one's feet. "Did Shakespeare spell his name with
an *e* at the end?" asked my brother. "I believe," said
I—but my father interrupted: "I very much doubt
if he used the Italian calligraphy *at all*." A certain
church in Belfast has both a Greek inscription over
the door and a curious tower. "That church is a
great landmark," said I, "I can pick it out from all
sorts of places—even from the top of Cave Hill."
"Such nonsense," said my father, "how could you
make out Greek letters three or four miles away?"

One conversation, held several years later, may be
recorded as a specimen of these continual cross-
purposes. My brother had been speaking of a re-
union dinner for the officers of the Nth Division
which he had lately attended. "I suppose your friend
Collins was there," said my father.

B. Collins? Oh no. He wasn't in the Nth, you
   know.

F. (After a pause.) Did these fellows not like Collins then?

B. I don't quite understand. What fellows?

F. The Johnnies that got up the dinner.

B. Oh no, not at all. It was nothing to do with
   liking or not liking. You see, it was a purely
   Divisional affair. There'd be no question of
   asking anyone who hadn't been in the Nth.

F. (After a long pause.) Hm! Well, I'm sure poor
   Collins was very much hurt.

There are situations in which the very genius of Fil-
ial Piety would find it difficult not to let some sign
of impatience escape him.

LOST FATHERS

I can't remember my father at all.   CLIVE JAMES

My father had left us when I was about five years old. I think he sold medical supplies. I was brought up by my mother.   LAUREN BACALL

As the only child of a father killed in Europe at the end of World War II, I can't help but take war personally. My dad was twenty-seven years old at the time of his death, and though there survives one photograph (on leave, before his final tour of duty) in which he's holding me in his arms, I have no conscious sense of him. Rather, over the years he coalesced for me as an amalgam of familiar anecdotes: a young man who could do the rumba, a soldier who once had his uniform altered by a tailor so that it would fit better, a first date, according to my mother, who "knew how to order" in a restaurant.

It's not much to go on. To those who didn't know him directly he's a compromise of his quirkier qualities, indistinct, better remembered for his death (my grandmother still wears a gold star on her best coat) than for his brief life.

My father was a bit player on the edges of the movie frame, the one who didn't make it back, whose fatality added anonymous atmosphere and a sense of mayhem. His grave, in a military cemetary near Tacoma, is located by graph paper like a small town on a map: E-9. He's frozen in age, kid in a T-shirt, a pair of dog tags stored in a box in my closet. His willingness to die for his country may have contributed in some small part to the fall of the Nazis, but more in the way of a pawn exchanged for its counterpart, two lives eliminated with the result that there were two fewer people in combat.

MICHAEL DORRIS

My dad was in the army. World War II. He got his college education from the army. After World War II he became an insurance salesman. Really, I didn't know my dad very well.　　AL PACINO

We were all destroyed by *Father Knows Best*. Nobody ever called me Kitten and pulled me on his lap when I cried about not being invited to the prom. I saw my father once a year. My father had children because they were a by-product of sex. And I think he's glad to have them, but I think he's sort of bewildered by it.   CARRIE FISHER of her father, Eddie Fisher

I don't expect to hear from him on my birthday or Christmas. I see him when I see him. He's like a ghost.

    JAMIE LEE CURTIS of her father, Tony Curtis

I would have liked to have a father.

    BARBRA STREISAND

My father wasn't there like most fathers, but, in a way, that can be a blessing. Familiarity breeds contempt, right?

    JACK FORD of his father, Gerald Ford

I never met him. He died 124 days before I was born.

    JOHN CLARK GABLE of his father, Clark Gable

Not much later, we sat down to eat. Then we heard this "pop." It was like no other "pop" I'd ever heard. Not like the gunfire you hear in the movies during "Cowboys and Indians" or "Cops and Robbers." It was a very small "pop," like a cap pistol. Mom and I looked at each other and instantly knew. When we rushed into the bedroom, we saw Dad lying on the bed, the gun slack in his hand. He had shot himself behind his right temple.   MARIETTE HARTLEY

My father is dead. And he had a terrible life. Because, at the bottom of his heart, he believed what people said about him. He believed he was a "nigger."
JAMES BALDWIN

When I was nine years old, my father died. It hurt more than the time I got my foot caught in the spoke of my bicycle—and took twice as long to heal.
ERMA BOMBECK

My father died just as I became an adult. . . . It's a tough thing because you've kind of known this guy as a child and then, just at the point where you start to understand where he's coming from, he's gone. So now you look back and he almost becomes a mythical person to you.   JOE MANTEGNA

My father died a difficult and terrible death . . . God grants an easy death only to the just.
SVETLANA ALILUYEVA of her father,
Joseph Stalin

My father was a hydropathist. . . . He dismissed the surgeon I had brought him and proceeded to cure himself with water, until he died several days later of lockjaw.
WASHINGTON ROEBLING of his father,
John A. Roebling

I stood numbly in front of the junior jailer, holding the small bundle that was all that was left of my father. The scent of his cologne was still on his clothes, the scent of *Shalimar*. I hugged his *shalwar* to me, suddenly remembering Kathleen Kennedy, who had worn her father's parka at Radcliffe long after the senator had been killed. Our two families had always been compared in terms of politics. Now we had a new and dreadful bond. That night and for many others, I, too, tried to keep my father near me by sleeping with his shirt under my pillow.

BENAZIR BHUTTO

My father's dying when I was very young created the obvious problems we all read about when we first learn to spell psychology. I first invented him, using little more than a handful of memories so fragmented they were like strobe-light freeze frames in the theater.

Later I began casting about for surrogates. As I settled into journalism I took my father figures from the older men along the way—editors, executives, always authority figures, never reporters; reporters are footloose, irresponsible corsairs according to the newspaper myth of my youth. One wanted to be a reporter. They were the romantic devils. But one would not have wanted a reporter for a father. So I tended toward bosses.

Rather late in the day, I realized that I had been a somewhat inferior father. Looking back on events, I realized that I had never been much interested in being a father. Of course I loved the children, but nowadays I see fathers whose lives are to some extent devoted to careers in fatherhood. They study the role, live it as a role and take pride in doing it well, suffer when they do it inadequately.

It never occurred to me to take fatherhood so seriously. Though I had children, I remained a son while my children were growing up. Offhand I don't know when I finally quit searching for a father. But I did, and I slowly and quietly realized that I had turned into the father figure I'd spent my life seeking, and that I wasn't cutting a very good one for my children. I am still not very good at it. The role doesn't come naturally to me. I feel like an impostor, and I laugh privately at myself faking it. Being eternal son was better. RUSSELL BAKER

Even now, twenty-one years after my father died, not a week goes by that I don't find myself thinking I should call him. HERB GARDNER

He was an upsetting man. His voice could be volcanic. It would sometimes crash through the world of comfort he had created for himself: suede shoes, tweed jackets, Of-Thee-I-Sing cologne, cigarettes in every cigarette box. Now, I know there was fear in his voice; but, unable to read it then, the sound was simply stamped on our imaginations as Authority. He surrounded us with toys, and answered every one of our material needs. He protected us. Jane and I never knew there had been a world war until we entered grade school.

My father was aloof. A game of catch in the park was two or three tosses. I did not know he worried; he simply cast no aura over the household. Even the birthday cards and Christmas presents from him were written in Mother's hand.

JOHN LAHR of his father, Bert Lahr

When I was a boy, my father's silence was one of the great mysteries of my life. Not only did he fail to answer when I spoke to him, he didn't even seem to hear me. There was no sign, no flicker in his face, to show that I had spoken, and I sometimes wondered whether I actually had. I used to stand there and listen, trying to catch the echo of my voice.

If I could have got my father's eye, could have looked him squarely in the face, I might have compelled him to answer me, or at least to acknowledge that I had spoken, but it was impossible to do this because he had a way of turning his head to one side, like a horse. I would walk around him, like someone circling a statue in a museum. Just as in medieval paintings people hold their heads to one side, so in my memory my father's face is always turned.

There came a time at last when he couldn't look away. He was in a hospital bed and it would have been too painful to turn his head because the illness had spread to his bones. When I placed myself in his line of sight, he had to see me.

It was our last chance to talk and I felt all that I had to say thrilling along my nerves. I had a lifetime of small and large talk saved up. I took a great breath, opened my mouth like an opera singer, but only a sigh came out, because talk doesn't keep. Evérything was concreted into lumps, like stuff left too long in the refrigerator. At the very end, I told my father that I would miss him. I did not say that I had always missed him.   ANATOLE BROYARD

Mona Simpson

from

The Lost Father

The last place I saw him was a Los Angeles restaurant that same year. It was the Hamburger Hamlet and I'm embarrassed, even now, that it wasn't someplace better. I've heard of divorced dads who took their daughters for hundred-dollar days. The daughter could pick out anything she wanted up to a hundred dollars. I would have wanted to eat in a ballroom with a quartet, but I never would have said so. I imagined waiters who would bring silver dishes they opened with a flourish at the end, their hands in gloves. Me in an ice-blue gown and long white gloves. I wanted my father to give me a velvet box, with a ring inside. I thought that would make me feel like his daughter.

I was never a fancy child. I didn't have velvet slippers and sequiny things. I didn't put my hair up different ways. I was always too embarrassed to be that. I wanted to be but I thought if people looked at me that way they'd laugh. It seemed like they had laughed at my mother once long ago before I was

born, and that was when she sealed up herself and
learned to shrug and just say, they don't know, they
don't know at all, these people around here, what I
have in me.

It was only a weekday morning and I was sick. So
far in California, my mother had left me alone when
I was sick. She had to. She had to go to work. But
now, since we'd seen my father that one time, she
wanted to call him.

"Don't," I said. I really didn't want her to. I didn't
know him that well. He seemed like too much work.

"If he wants to be your father, let him do what
fathers do for a change."

"Don't. Please."

But then she called and he was coming and I had
to get dressed. I already understood that you had to
look nice for men. Any time. It wasn't like being at
home with women. I fought on tights and shoes.
Standing up, I looked normal but I felt sick at the
back of my neck.

It was a weekday morning and so I guess he wasn't
working. He hadn't really told us. My mother figured Uta was supporting him. "Are you kidding,
why else do you think he's with her?" I waited,
dressed up in my best dress, collapsed in our corner
chair. I felt like being in bed, not hot and dressed
up, the comb pressed through my limp, sick-day
hair. But also, I knew I'd better not miss a chance
with my father. I couldn't tell how many more
chances I would get.

My mother was gone by the time he arrived. I
unlocked the door and let him in. "Hungry?" he
said, standing there. His keys dangled off the end
of his right hand.

We drove to the Hamburger Hamlet my mother
and I went to all the time for dinner. It was an odd

time of day, though. And my father asked the hostess to give us a booth in the bar. I'd never sat in the bar part before. TV voices were mumbling in the background and we sat in the dark. I kept an empty place on my left side. I didn't know where to put my hands, with my father. They seemed wrong everywhere. I sat on them.

"Coffee black," he ordered like my mother always did. They said it with a kind of air. Coffee with milk was tawdry, something housewives drank.

Now that I am grown up, I understand how hard it is to talk to children. Sometimes you just want relief. But he and I, we didn't light up once that day. I was too tired to help him much. Usually I helped. Then he drove me home and left, telling me to lock the door from the inside. I heard his shuffling footsteps on the landing, then his car, and I took my good clothes off, not hanging them up, leaving them like petals just where they dropped, and fell nude and slender and hot under the quilt and slept. It was a quilt my grandmother had made on her gray living room carpet. I'd helped her measure with my hands and tied the yarns.

That was the last time I saw my father. It was a weekday in 1970, in Los Angeles. It took me a while to understand that that was the last time I would see him. I don't think he knew this at the time either.

Three weeks later, we hadn't heard from him and so my mother called the number in Pasadena he had written down. The operator told us it had been disconnected and there was no new number. I called 411 for every city and town in southern California. None of them found him either.

I decided if I ever saw him again he would not be my father, but just a man.

Patti Davis

from

The Way I See It

I can't remember the exact dialogue, but it was along the lines of: My mother was embarrassed to be seen with me, with my hair falling over one eye, Veronica Lake style, my overdone makeup, and my tight jeans. And, of course, my attitude—"chip on her shoulder a mile high"—an observation directed to my father as if I weren't there. My father was baffled, uncomfortable with dissension in the ranks.

The final blow came when I pulled my hair back, exposed my newly pierced ears, and said, "Since you're getting upset, you might as well get upset about this, too. I pierced my ears."

My mother seethed, I stood defiant, and my father said, "Well, before you get your appendix out, do you think you could let us know in advance?" My father always makes jokes when he feels there is tension in the air. Sometimes, it would help, but not then. My mother turned on her heels, announced that she was going to sit in the car for the rest of the afternoon, and walked off. That left my father and me standing there awkwardly, facing each other, close but miles apart. I realized then that we only knew how to relate to each other by bouncing off my mother. Ours is a ricochet relationship. In some way, she has to be there or we've lost each other.

I remember, on that day, that the minutes stretched out interminably. With people all around us, we stood there floundering—two lonely souls with nothing to say.

My father has a scar on his thumb—a dent, really, on the tip, which he says came from a childhood accident when he and his brother were playing with an ax. I've always loved that scar; when I was a child, I used to touch it, although I don't think my father noticed. It made him seem more real to me; it was something tangible, something that said, "I was a kid once, too. I got in trouble, almost lost my thumb." Because there are so many incongruities in my father. Even his hands—they're pale, soft, not rugged at all, not as large as you might expect. But then there's that scar.

And that's what I remember most about standing in the barnyard with him on Parents' Day, with my mother sitting a hundred yards away in the car, windows rolled up on her anger. His hand went up to his face, to smooth his hair or something, and I stared at it until he became a little more real to me. A kid once—"almost lost my thumb."

"Patti, you can't let your mother sit in the car all day," he said finally.

"Well, what am I supposed to do?"

He hesitated, not sure for a second exactly what the best course of action was. "Well, I think you should go apologize."

I did, but only because I preferred the engagement of battle to the disengagement of someone I wanted to be close to, but couldn't find. The scar on his thumb has told me more than anything else about my father.

Cyra McFadden

from

Rain or Shine

When my father died, in April of 1980, newspapers in the west compared him with John Wayne. "Cy Taillon was more than a rodeo announcer," said the writer for the Miles City *Star* in Miles City, Montana, "like John Wayne was more than an actor. Each became an embodiment of an ideal, a spokesman for a quality of life and a way of living it." America was younger when my father left his family's North Dakota farm and Wayne left the football field of the University of Southern California, the writer continued. "It took men of iron will, stout hearts and sensitive manner to tame her. Stubborn men who spoke their minds and minded what they spoke. Times have changed, so has America. And so has rodeo."

He's right about America and rodeo. My father never changed, not in his loyalty to Western values. When his Denver house was burglarized of two hundred dollars' worth of appliances several years ago, he told the Denver *Post,* "I plan to have an armed resident in the house with orders to shoot first and argue later."

Cy was at the top of his profession then. In fact, he was the top, with no competition for his title "Dean of Rodeo Announcers," an accolade accorded him by the rest of the rodeo world and almost always attached to his name. Once a rakehell, he'd been respected and respectable for thirty years: well paid, happily married, a family man and a householder. But inside him, beneath his custom-tailored Western jackets, beat the heart of a cowboy. No one stole his toaster while he was out on the road, if he could help it, and walked away intact. A shotgun shell or two should handle the problem nicely.

We were not speaking to each other then. His blue-eyed darling as a child, named after him, dressed like him as a wrong-sex, unusually short cowboy, I'd grown up, moved away from Montana, moved away in heart and mind from my father and shoot first, argue later. I had a couple of degrees, a divorce behind me and a second marriage; a suburban California house; belonged to the ACLU; took part in San Francisco peace marches while my half brother by my father's second marriage was fighting in Vietnam and my father editorializing from the crow's nest, the rodeo announcer's booth, in support of the war.

The last time we'd seen each other, he and I argued about racial intermarriage, hippies, Catholicism as the one true religion and what to have for dinner. We were at an elegant San Francisco Chinese restaurant. My father insisted that we both eat chow mein. I was full of self and my new sophistication and didn't want to sit at the same table with a man who'd order chow mein at Kan's. Especially a man in kangaroo-skin cowboy boots, nipped-in Western suit and diamond pinkie ring.

We were obnoxious in equal proportions, but my father won. He had a voice that could fill a football stadium without amplification, and he was picking up the check.

So he went back to embodying the West while I went back to ACLU meetings. We exchanged letters in which we discussed politics and each other's character defects. Then we exchanged no letters at all, keeping track of each other through relatives, waiting for the other to heal the rift. Cy Taillon's daughter, I am as stubborn as he was. We loved each other, missed each other, and made ourselves miserable, and this went on for years, time for our grievances to harden into granite.

I rankled at a distance about the form my father's letters took, when I was still receiving them. He sent me a carbon of the letters he wrote his entire family. It was a large family. He always sent me the blurry last carbon.

His own grievances predated our quarrel about San Francisco and whether or not it was part Sodom, part Gomorrah. As a child, I used to meet my father on the rodeo circuit in the summers, in Billings or Miles City or Lewiston, traveling by Greyhound bus, a label pinned to my shirt; "If bus isn't met deliver to Cy Taillon, fairgrounds." On each such occasion, he marched me off instantly to a beauty shop to have a permanent wave, frustrated beyond tolerance that no matter who did what to me, and no matter how much he paid for it, my hair refused to curl. He wanted a daughter who looked like Shirley Temple. Instead, he had a sulky, waiflike child who looked more like Oliver Twist.

The afternoon before we met for dinner at Kan's,

he'd made one more attempt. "Go get your hair done," he said, and gave me twenty dollars. At the beauty shop in his San Francisco hotel, a hairdresser tormented me into a lofty bouffant. I felt freakish, and it didn't help our relations that my father was once again disappointed. "I give up," he said when he saw me. I had to put on my dark glasses. Crying, I had been taught long ago, was for sissies.

We were a long time reconciling, and when reconciliation came, it came on my father's terms. He was sick and demoralized after a small stroke. A letter turned up in my mailbox, on his flamboyant stationery, with its cowboy hat, microphone and lariat logo and the legend: "Cy Taillon, Master of Ceremonies and Rodeo Announcer, with records unequaled for consecutive engagements." He wrote that he'd been hoping for a move from me for years, feeling that "any desire to communicate" should originate with me because he was blameless in our estrangement.

I raged at his tone of injured merit; thought about how he always told reporters he had two children, my two half brothers, Terry and Tommy, and not three; remembered every hurt, every slight, and how, when Cy finally left his tempestuous marriage to my mother, he quickly began the process of erasing me from the record of his life along with her.

When we were together, he sometimes slipped and called me "Pat." I was the living reminder that he'd once slept with her, caroused with her, been deeply and destructively in love with her. Respectability had come late and hard to him. I remembered the person he'd been—dazzling, reckless, a drunk.

The day his letter came, I phoned him, and the voice that had made him famous resonated over the line. Majestically, he told me that if I apologized, he was willing to forgive me. He was, he said, incapable of holding a grudge.

We had nine years to make our peace before cancer killed him. I wrote a book during that time, was interviewed by reporters myself and began to tell the ones who asked me where I got my odd name that my father invented it. He was Cy Taillon, Dean of the Rodeo Announcers and living Western legend.

Itabari Njeri

from

Every Good-bye
Ain't Gone

Daddy wore boxer shorts when he worked; that's all.
He'd sit for hours reading and writing at a long,
rectangular table covered with neat stacks of *I.F.
Stone's Weekly, The Nation, The New Republic,* and the
handwritten pages of his book in progress, *The To-
lono Station and Beyond.* A Mott's applesauce jar filled
with Teacher's scotch was a constant, and his own
forerunner of today's wine coolers was the ever present chaser: ginger ale and Manischewitz Concord
grape wine in a tall, green iced-tea glass.

As he sat there, his beer belly weighing down the
waistband of his shorts, I'd watch. I don't know if
he ever saw me. I hid from him at right angles.
From the bend of the hallway, at the end of a long,
dark, L-shaped corridor in our Harlem apartment,
it was at least thirty feet to the living room where
my father worked, framed by the doorway. I sat
cross-legged on the cold linoleum floor and in-
spected his seated, six-foot-plus figure through a
telescope formed by my forefinger and thumb: bare

feet in thonged sandals, long hairy legs that rose toward the notorious shorts (I hated those shorts, wouldn't bring my girlfriends home because of those shorts), breasts that could fill a B cup, and a long neck on which a balding head rested. Viewed in isolation, I thought perhaps I'd see him clearer, know him better.

Daddy was a philosopher, a Marxist historian, an exceptional teacher, and a fine tenor. He had a good enough voice to be as great a concert artist as John McCormack, one of his favorites. The obstacles to that career couldn't have been much greater than the ones he actually overcame.

The state of Georgia, where my father grew up, established its version of the literacy test in 1908, the year he was born. If you substituted Georgia for Mississippi in the story that Lerone Bennett Jr. relates in *Before the Mayflower: A History of Black America*, the main character could easily have been my father: A black teacher, a graduate of Eton and Harvard, presents himself to a Mississippi registrar. The teacher is told to read the state constitution and several books. He does. The registrar produces a passage in Greek, which the teacher reads. Then another in Latin. Then other passages in French, German, and Spanish, all of which the teacher reads. The registrar finally holds up a page of Chinese characters and asks: "What does this mean?" The teacher replies: "It means you don't want me to vote."

Apocryphal, perhaps, but the tale exemplified enough collective experience that I heard my father tell virtually the same story about a former Morehouse College classmate to a buddy over the phone one afternoon. At the punchline, he fell into a fit of laughter, chuckling hard into a balled fist he held at his mouth. Finally, he said, "Fred, I'll have to call you back," then fell back on the bed, in his boxer shorts, laughing at the ceiling.

He claimed he burst out laughing like this once in a class at Harvard. A law professor, discussing some constitutional issue in class, singled out my father and said, "In this matter, regarding men of your race—"

"Which race is that?" my father boomed, cutting him off, "the fifty yard or the one hundred?" But it seemed to me he always related that particular tale with a sneer on his lips.

He'd been at Harvard studying law on a postdoctoral scholarship from 1942 to 1943. After receiving his Ph.D. in philosophy from the University of Toronto ten years earlier, he had headed toward the dust bowls others were escaping in the mid-1930s and became the editor of a black newspaper, the *Oklahoma Eagle,* in Tulsa. He eventually returned to academia and by 1949 was the head of the philosophy department at Morgan State University in Baltimore. That's where he met my mother, a nurse many years his junior.

My mother—who commits nothing to paper, speaks of the past cryptically, and believes all unpleasantries are best kept under a rug—once leaked the fact that she and my father took me to a parade in Brooklyn when I was about three. We were standing near the arch at Grand Army Plaza when he suddenly hauled off and punched her in the mouth, with me in her arms. My mother, a very gentle and naive woman, said the whole thing left her in a state of shock. My father had never been violent before.

They separated, and I seldom saw my father again until my parents reunited when I was seven. We

moved into my father's six-room apartment on
129th Street, between Convent Avenue and St. Nich-
olas Terrace. It was certainly far more spacious than
the apartment I'd lived in with my mother on St.
James Place in Brooklyn. The immediate neighborhood was an attractive, hilly section of Harlem, just
a few blocks from City College. All things considered, I hated it. More precisely, I hated my father,
so I hated it all.

Because of his past leftist political affiliations,
Daddy had lost his government and university jobs.
Now, out of necessity but also desire, he decided to
devote his time to teaching younger people. He
wanted to reach them at a stage in their lives when
he felt he could make a difference. He joined the
faculty of a Jersey City high school and began teaching journalism, history, and English. He also taught
English at night to foreign-born students at City College. His students, I came to learn, loved him; his
daughter found it hard to. I made the mistake of
calling him Pop—once. He said, "Don't ever call me
that again. If you don't like calling me Daddy, you
can call me Dr. Moreland."

Once, my mother deserted me, leaving me alone
with him. She went to Atlanta for several weeks with
my baby brother to tend my ailing Grandma Hattie,
my father's mother. Since I hadn't known this man
most of my seven years on the planet, and didn't
like him much now that I did, I asked him if I could
stay around the corner with a family friend, Aunt
Pearl. "If she asks you to stay, fine. But don't ask
her," he told me. Naturally I asked her.

When he asked me if I had asked her, I hesitated.
But I was not a child inclined to lie. So I said, "I
don't want to lie. I asked her." I got a beating for

that, a brutal beating with a belt that left welts and bruises on my legs for months.

My father felt children should be hit for any infraction. Further, they should be seen and not heard, speak only when spoken to, etc. From the day he hit me, the latter became my philosophy, too. I never consciously decided to stop speaking to my father, but for the next ten years, I rarely initiated a conversation with him. Later he would tell me, "You were a very strange child."

But if I would not accept him as a father, my curiosity would not let me deny him as a teacher. One day, a question about the nature of truth compelled a thaw in my emotional cold war—nothing less could have. Truth changes, a classmate in the seventh grade had insisted that day. It is constant, I argued, and went to my father for confirmation.

People's perceptions change, I explained. New information debunks the lies of the past, but the truth was always there. And I told my father what I had told my mostly white classmates in a Bronx junior high school at the height of the civil rights movement: Black people were always human beings worthy of the same rights other Americans enjoyed, but it took hundreds of years of a slave system that dehumanized the master as well as the slave and a social revolution before most white Americans would accept that truth.

My father turned from his worktable, took off his glasses, with their broken right temple piece, and released a long and resonant "Yesssss." And then he spoke to me of a rational cosmos and what Lincoln had to do with Plato. When our philosophical discussion ended, we each went to our separate corners.

*   *   *

My father had a beaten, black upright piano in the parlor, badly out of tune. But its bench was a treasure of ancient sheet music: Vincent Youman's "Through the Years," with a picture of Gladys Swarthout on the frayed cover. And I loved the chord changes to "Spring Is Here."

I ventured from the sanctuary of my blue-walled room one summer afternoon, walking down the long hallway toward the kitchen, then stopped abruptly. I heard my father in the kitchen several feet away; he was making an ice-cream soda, something as forbidden to him as alcohol since he was a diabetic. I heard the clink of a metal spoon against a glass as he sang, "For I lately took a notion for to cross the briny ocean, and I'm off to Philadelphia in the morning." It was an Irish folk song made famous by John McCormack. I backed up. Too late. He danced across the kitchen threshold in his boxer shorts, stopped when he spotted me in the shadows, then shook his head. He smiled, lifted one leg and both arms in a Jackie Gleason "and away we go" motion, then slid off.

Minutes later he called me. "Jill the Pill, you know this song?" I knew all the songs and wrote down the words to "Moon River" for him. Then he asked me to sing it. I was always ready to sing, even for my father.

He sat on the edge of his bed with the lyrics in his hand as I sang. When I finished the phrase "We're after the same rainbow's end, waitin' round the bend, my huckleberry friend," my daddy looked at me and said what others would tell me years later but with far less poetry: "My girl, you have the celestial vibration." And then he asked me to sing it again and told me it was "wonderful." Then I left him.

*   *   *

For days, maybe weeks, a tense calm would reign in the apartment. Then, without warning, the hall would fill with harsh voices. My father stood in the narrow, shadowy space hitting my mother. "Put it down," he yelled. "Put it down or I'll . . ."

My mother had picked up a lamp in a lame effort to ward off his blows. His shouting had awakened me. I'd been sick in bed with the flu and a high fever. When he saw me open my bedroom door he yelled, "Get back in your room." I did, my body overtaken by tremors and the image of my mother branded on my eyeballs. I swore that I would never let anyone do that to me or to anyone else I had the power to help. I had no power to help my mother. It was an oath with terrible consequences, one I'd have to disavow to permit myself the vulnerability of being human.

I know my father's fury was fueled by his sense of insignificance. He felt himself to be an intellectual giant boxed in by mental midgets. Unlike Ralph Ellison, Paul Robeson, or Richard Wright—all contemporaries and acquaintances of my father's—he was never acknowledged by the dominant culture whose recognition he sought. He could be found, Ellison once told me, pontificating in Harlem barbershops, elucidating the dialogues of Plato for a captive audience of draped men, held prone, each with a straight-edge razor pressed against his cheek.

My father's unreconciled identities—the classic schizophrenia of being black and an American, the contradictions of internalizing whole the cultural values of a society that sees you, when it sees you at all, as life in one of its lower forms—stoked his alcoholism. And since my father at once critiqued the society that denied him and longed for its approbation, he lived with the pain-filled consciousness of one who knows he is a joke. I think sometimes he laughed the hardest, so often did I stumble upon him alone, chuckling into his balled fist at some silent, invisible comedian.

When his drunken rages ended, he slept for days, spread out on the bed wearing only his boxer shorts. I watched him on those days, too, daring to come closer, safe with the knowledge that Morpheus held him. I examined his face, wondering who he was and why he was. As I watched, he'd lift his head off the pillow, then fall back muttering: "Truth and justice will prevail."

DADDY
DEAREST

I grew up thinking my father would one day kill me.
I never remember a time when I was not afraid of
my father's hands except for those bright, palmy
years when Dad was waging war or serving in carrier-
based squadrons overseas. I used to pray that
America would go to war or for Dad to get overseas
assignments that would take him to Asian cities I'd
never heard of. Ironically, a time of war for the
United States became both respite and separate
peace for my family. When my father was off killing
the enemy, his family slept securely, and not because
he was making the world safe for democracy.

PAT CONROY

My dad, he did my mom wrong. He left us, he beat
my mother up all the time. He shot my mom, left
her with a mark on her leg. He made my mom work
two jobs, and he just left his responsibilities behind.
I can never forgive that. Why should I? I know

where he is. I hope he reads this, because if he ever decides to come out of the woodwork, I'll be ready for him. I'll have some fun then.

Everything is about that. I look at my opponent and I see my dad, so I have to take him out. I have to kill him. I'll do anything I have to do to get him out of there.   JAMES TONEY, JR.

[My father] lay down on the bed and gave me a razor strap and he said, "Hit me harder." And that hurt me more than getting the beating myself. I couldn't do it. I just broke down and cried.

TED TURNER

[He] yelled and screamed the whole time. It was a nightmare. So when we had finished and we were just going down the Chattahoochee River and Dad said, "Well, did everybody have a great time?" I said no. And boy, he smacked me hard.

TED TURNER, JR.

Once, when I was a teenager, he wanted to tutor me in fractions and the first time I didn't get it, he kind of got a little nervous. The second time I didn't get it, he started swearing. The third time, he pulled his hair. The fourth time, he gave me a little bump on the shoulder out of frustration; he didn't mean to hit me. He was just as shocked as I was. That's the only time he ever hit me.

PAUL HOWARD of his father, Moe Howard

My father was an eccentric, extremely conservative Frenchman who deplored most aspects of the twentieth century, particularly the laxness of its education. And according to his wishes, I spent my first nine years confined to my room, tutored at home by a governess quite as tyrannical as my father. She was a rabid hypochondriac, convinced that the mere *sight* of another child might lead me to catch some deadly germ . . . I lived in extreme isolation. Once a week we commuted to a correspondence school where I'd receive the assignments for the following week—typically French, didactic, desiccating assignments, memorizing Latin verbs and the dates of battles won by Napoleon. But when I was eight years old an unprecedented event took place—a new teacher came in and gave us the following assignment: "Write a Story About Anything You Wish." I was filled with excitement and anguish by this novel freedom. I began as a severe minimalist. Here's the cautionary tale I wrote: "The little girl was forbidden by her parents to walk alone to the lake at the other end of the green lawn. But she wished to visit a green-eyed frog who could offer her the key to freedom. One day she disobeyed her parents and walked to the lake, and was immediately drowned. The End." The following day, during his daily visit to the study room my father perused the composition and raised a storm. "Pathetic dribble! You dare call that a story? What will become of you if you don't ever finish anything!" And he grabbed the paper from my little desk and tore it to shreds. It was a May evening in 1939, fourteen months before he died in the Resistance. My father had been the love of my life, and he'd warned me that I should never write again. I didn't attempt fiction again for over thirty years.   FRANCINE DU PLESSIX GRAY

He yelled constantly, especially at me, which is my earliest recollection of him. He even dropped me in my infancy on the concrete sidewalk outside our apartment. The large welt that appeared disappeared after a few days, but it's possible I suffered brain damage as a result.   BRIAN WILSON

My father and I were always on the most distant terms when I was a boy—a sort of armed neutrality, so to speak. At irregular intervals this neutrality was broken and suffering ensued; but I will be candid enough to say that the breaking and suffering were always divided with strict impartiality between us— which is to say, my father did the breaking and I did the suffering.   MARK TWAIN

The son of a bitch left us dangling from the brink of insecurity over the pit of poverty. What on God's good earth was there for me to love about my father? Or even admire?   ALEXANDER WOOLLCOTT

My father was a compulsive gambler. He was smart, he was funny, he had a personality that could fill the room, but he would gamble the rent money on a baseball game.   BOB COSTAS

David Letterman said he'd heard that my father sang everywhere, and I said, "Yes, the world is his shower." And often he likes to use women for soap.
CARRIE FISHER of her father, Eddie Fisher

I have always thought that the initial trouble between me and my father was that he couldn't see the slightest purpose in my existence.
LAURENCE OLIVIER

My father did not like me. My presence was insistently physical. He was a fastidious man. He dusted the chair on which the cat had been lying before occupying it himself. He ate a banana with a knife and fork—to modern minds a dead giveaway if ever there was one. In later years I had to supply various subsidiary kinds of fuel for the furnaces of his hatred. In infancy my existence was enough.
QUENTIN CRISP

They had come to a standoff in the living room. His shouting made my hair stand on end. I could see that my mother was trembling and trying to hide her tears. I scrambled between them and faced my father. Thrusting my chin forward, I spit out my words. "I know who pays for the groceries around here!"

I had touched his masculine pride. There was a terrible silence as my mother disappeared out the door. I watched my father go into the kitchen and open a drawer. He pulled out a knife and turned toward me, saying, "You little . . ."

The expression on his face was as terrifying as the

knife. As he came at me, I rushed behind the dining room table. He hesitated. Maybe he had second thoughts. I was quick enough to beat him out the door of the apartment.　　GELSEY KIRKLAND

My father is a mechanical person. He always tried to save money by working on everybody's cars. And my older brothers would go out and work with him. He would tell them to hand him a nine-sixteenths wrench and they'd to it. I'd get out there and he'd say give me a nine-sixteenths wrench and I didn't know what the hell he was talking about. He used to get irritated with me and say, "You don't know what the hell you're doing, go on in there with the women."　　MICHAEL JORDAN

My father was a wicked man—a very wicked man.
　　KATE PERUGINI of her father, Charles Dickens

My old man made The Great Santini look like Leo Buscaglia.　　DENNIS MILLER

He was a total control monster.
　　CELESTE ERHARD of her father, Werner Erhard

I never forgave my father for being a bigot.
NORMAN LEAR

That morning I had come up as usual at eleven, and a strange gentleman and my father were talking together near the companion. As I appeared my father gave me a frown to go below, but the stranger caught sight of me and laughing called me. I came to them and the stranger was surprised on hearing I could swim. "Jump in, Jim!" cried my father, "and swim round."

Nothing loath, I ran down the ladder, pulled off my clothes and jumped in. The stranger and my father were above me smiling and talking; my father waved his hand and I swam round the vessel. When I got back, I was about to get on the steps and come aboard when my father said:

"No, no, swim on round till I tell you to stop."

Away I went again quite proud, but when I got round the second time I was tired; I had never swum so far and I had sunk deep in the water and a little spray of wave had gone into my mouth; I was very glad to get near the steps, but as I stretched out my hand to mount them, my father waved his hand.

"Go on, go on," he cried, "till you're told to stop!"

I went on; but now I was very tired and frightened as well, and as I got to the bow the sailors leant over the bulwark and one encouraged me: "Go slow, Jim; you'll get round all right." I saw it was big Newton, the stroke-oar of my father's gig, but just because of his sympathy I hated my father the more for making me so tired and so afraid.

When I got round the third time, I swam very slowly and let myself sink very low, and the stranger spoke for me to my father, and then he himself told me to "come up."

I came eagerly, but a little scared at what my father might do, but the stranger came over to me, saying: "He's all blue; that water's very cold, Captain; someone should give him a good towelling."

My father said nothing but: "Go down and dress," adding, "get warm."

The memory of my fear made me see that he was always asking me to do too much, and I hated him who could get drunk and shame me and make me run races up the rigging with the cabin boys who were grown men and could beat me. I disliked him.

FRANK HARRIS

My father does not take a particular interest or pride in what I do. If he has seen any of the films, he certainly hasn't told me, except when *Last Temptation of Christ* was coming along. Then I started getting phone calls from him, asking what theaters it was going to be in, how many, what the release dates were, et cetera. After his second or third call I started figuring it out, and I said: "Dad, are you involved in this movement to block my film?" And he said, "Yes, but only locally. Just to keep it out of my town."

PAUL SCHRADER

He can't read my stuff, he claims, because he can't follow it.

MARTIN AMIS of his father, Kingsley Amis

I spent many hours ... with Father, but I don't remember his talking much. I would ask him to read me the funnies from the papers, and he would begin sometimes but soon give up, saying, "There's no use reading all that trash." All my life I had that feeling about Father, that he wanted me around out of pure possessiveness. The fact is that when Father was with me, he was inclined to be dry and censorious and negative.

PAUL MELLON of his father, Andrew W. Mellon

My father never liked me or my sister, and he never liked our mother either, after an initial infatuation, and in fact, he never liked anyone at all after an hour or two, no, no one except a stooge, someone he could depend on to be a lackey, a nitwit he could make fun of behind his back, someone he could control completely by whatever means he could make work—fear, intimidation, or, because he was a famous and admired man, blind worshipfulness.

And he wanted me and Lucy and my mother to die.

ARAM SAROYAN of his father, William Saroyan

It was 5:55 in the morning. I was standing in front of Westward Ho market on San Vicente Boulevard. I had dragged myself to the market because I needed a drink. Just a couple of nice cold beers to put out the fire in my stomach, and a little half-pint of tequila to still the rockslide in my head.

At six sharp a white-haired man got out of his car in the parking lot and joined me at the door to the market. He was wearing a bathrobe, was unshaven and bleary-eyed and needed a drink as much as I did. He looked me up and down. Even a smile hurt.

I squinted at him. It was a real effort to speak. So I didn't.

The manager opened the door and we went inside. We both padded softly to the liquor shelves, pulled down our favorite medicines, paid, and left. On the way out the older man turned to me. "Give us a call, huh, son? We'd love to see you."

"Sure, Pop," I said. I watched my father return to his car. He waved. I waved. He drove off. I slipped back to my apartment as swiftly and smoothly as possible, holding the bottles gingerly, as if they were condor eggs. We both knew I wouldn't call.

NED WYNN of his father, Keenan Wynn

For as long as I can remember, he got the biggest kick out of lurking around our windows at night and tapping on the glass, or pretending to break in. When one of us tiptoed to the window to investigate, my father, wearing a gruesome latex mask, leaped up and growled like a beast. We screamed in terror, and Joseph laughed. It wasn't done playfully or as part of a game. Why a grown man would deliberately scare his children out of their wits is beyond me.

Even worse was being startled awake by a hideous monster hovering just inches above our faces. While we shrieked, Joseph ripped off his mask and fell out laughing, as if this was the funniest thing he'd ever seen. It got to where every night I pulled the covers tightly over my head and gently rocked myself until drifting off. Even now, that is the only way I can get to sleep. LA TOYA JACKSON

During that extended period of rage that goes by the name of my adolescence, what terrified me most about my father was not the violence I expected him momentarily to unleash upon me, but the violence I wished every night at the dinner table to commit upon his ignorant, barbaric carcass. How I wanted to send him howling from the land of the living when he ate from the serving bowl with his own fork, or sucked the soup from his spoon instead of waiting for it to cool, or attempted, God forbid, to express an opinion on any subject whatsoever.

PHILIP ROTH, *Portnoy's Complaint*

He was a very intimidating figure: six-foot-six, 240 pounds, a big, raw-boned, tough man. He was the only man I've ever been afraid of. When I did things that he didn't like, he was a very tough and physical disciplinarian. I think he probably had some demons within him from the war. He was in the middle of it—he didn't just peel potatoes, he killed people. I don't know what effect that had on him, but he would take an occasional drink and he would get a little physical. I learned from being on the receiving end how *not* to discipline my own kids.

KEN STABLER

When my sister or I did something really bad—like lying or breaking a piece of furniture—he'd put us to bed and threaten to make us go without dinner. He claimed this was more effective than spankings.

I don't know how effective it was, but it was certainly more pleasant, especially since, in all the years I was growing up, he never once carried out the threat about no dinner.

After I'd been incarcerated in the bedroom for a while, he'd open the door and say in a grim tone, "Do you think you can behave yourself from now on?"

I'd of course answer "Yes," and he'd reply, "All right. Put your clothes on and come down to dinner. I don't know why I should have to eat that dinner, and not you."

ARTHUR MARX of his father, Groucho Marx

I thought my name was Jesus Christ: "Jee-sus *Christ!*" And my brother Russell thought his name was Damnit: "Damn it, will you stop all that noise!" "Jee-sus *Christ,* shut up!" One day I'm out playing in the rain, my father said, "Damn it, will you get in here?!" I said, "Dad, I'm Jesus Christ."

BILL COSBY

Gay Talese

from

Unto the Sons

Back in the kitchen, sitting in front of a bowl of dry
cereal that his mother had left for him, he looked
at the headlines and photographs on the front pages
of the newspapers. One was an Italian-language
paper that he of course could not read; another was
The New York Times, which he refused to read because it did not have comics. But on this day he was
drawn to the front pages of these and other papers
because most of them displayed pictures of the dev-
astation left after recent air raids—smoke was rising
out of a large hilltop building that American bombers had attacked in Italy, and had completely destroyed. The headlines identified the ruins as the
Abbey of Monte Cassino, located in southern Italy,
northwest of Naples. The articles described the
abbey as very old, dating back to the sixth century.
They called it a cradle of learning throughout the
Dark Ages, a scholarly center for Benedictine monks,
who had occupied it for fourteen centuries; it was
built on a hill that Nazi soldiers had taken over dur-

ing the winter of 1943–1944. The raid on February
15, 1944, had involved more than a hundred forty
of America's heaviest bombers, the B-17 Flying For-
tresses; these, together with the medium-sized
bombers that followed, released nearly six hundred
tons of bombs on the abbey and its grounds. It was
the first time the Allies had deliberately made a tar-
get of a religious building.

After breakfast, while brushing his teeth in the
bathroom, dressed and ready to go down to the
store, Gay heard strange noises in the apartment, a
pounding on the walls and the cursing of an angry
male voice. When he opened the door, he saw his
father, in overcoat and hat, swatting down the model
airplanes suspended from Gay's bedroom ceiling by
almost invisible threads.

"Stop it, they're mine!" Gay screamed, horrified at
the sight of his carefully crafted American bombers
and fighter planes, framed with balsa wood and covered with crisp paper, being smashed into smither-
eens by his father. *"Stop, stop, stop—they're mine, get
out of my room, get out!"* Joseph did not seem to hear,
but kept swinging wildly with both hands until he
had knocked out of the air and crushed with his feet
every single plane that his son had for more than a
year taken countless evening hours to make. They
were two dozen in number—exact replicas of the
United States' most famous fighter planes and
bombers—the B-17 Flying Fortress, the B-26 Ma-
rauder, the B-25 Mitchell, the Bell P-39 Airacobra
fighter plane, the P-38 Lockheed Lightning, the P-
40 Kittyhawk; Britain's renowned Spitfire, Hurri-
cane, Lancaster; and other Allied models that until
this moment had been the proudest achievement of
Gay's boyhood.

"I hate you, I hate you," he cried at his father before running out of the apartment, and then down the side staircase to the first landing, where he grabbed his roller skates. "I hate you!" he yelled again, looking up toward the living room door, but seeing no sign of his father. Crying, he continued to the bottom of the staircase and out onto the avenue, then thrust his skates around his shoe tops without bothering to tighten them; and as quickly as he could, he headed up Asbury Avenue, thrashing his arms through the cold wind and sobbing as he sped between several bewildered people who suddenly stepped aside. As he passed the Russell Bakery Shop, he lost his balance and swerved toward the plate-glass window. People were lined up in front of the pastry counter, and two women screamed as they saw the boy, his hands outstretched, crash into the window and then fall bleeding with glass cascading down on his head.

Unconscious until the ambulance arrived, and then embarrassed by the crowds staring silently behind the ropes that the police held in front of the bakery's broken window, he turned toward his father, who was embracing him in bloody towels, crying and saying something in Italian that the boy did not understand.

"*Non ti spagnare,*" Joseph said, over and over—don't be afraid—using the old dialect of southern Italians who had lived in fear of the Spanish monarchy. "*Non ti spagnare,*" Joseph went on, cradling his son's head with his bloody hands, and closing his eyes as he heard his son repeating, tearfully, "I hate you."

Joseph then became silent, watching the ambulance crew arrive with a stretcher as the police ordered the people in the crowd to keep their distance.

When Joseph next spoke, he did so in English, although his son found him no less bewildering than before, even as Joseph repeated: "Those who love you, make you cry. . . ."

Mark Twain

from

Huckleberry Finn

I had shut the door to. Then I turned around, and there he was. I used to be scared of him all the time, he tanned me so much. I reckoned I was scared now, too; but in a minute I see I was mistaken—that is, after the first jolt, as you may say, when my breath sort of hitched, he being so unexpected; but right away after I see I warn't scared of him worth bothering about.

He was most fifty, and he looked it. His hair was long and tangled and greasy, and hung down, and you could see his eyes shining through like he was behind vines. It was all black, no gray; so was his long, mixed-up whiskers. There warn't no color in his face, where his face showed; it was white; not like another man's white, but a white to make a body sick, a white to make a body's flesh crawl—a tree-toad white, a fish-belly white. As for his clothes—just rags, that was all. He had one ankle resting on t'other knee; the boot on that foot was busted, and two of his toes stuck through, and he worked them now and then. His hat was laying on the floor—an old black slouch with the top caved in, like a lid.

I stood a-looking at him; he set there a-looking at me, with his chair tilted back a little. I set the candle down. I noticed the window was up; so he had clumb in by the shed. He kept a-looking me all over. By and by he says:

"Starchy clothes—very. You think you're a good deal of a big-bug, *don't* you?"

"Maybe I am, maybe I ain't," I says.

"Don't you give me none o' your lip," says he. "You've put on considerable many frills since I been away. I'll take you down a peg before I get done with you. You're educated, too, they say—can read and write. You think you're better'n your father, now, don't you, because he can't? *I'll* take it out of you. Who told you you might meddle with such hifa-lut'n foolishness, hey?—who told you you could?"

"The widow. She told me."

"The widow, hey?—and who told the widow she could put in her shovel about a thing that ain't none of her business?"

"Nobody never told her."

"Well, I'll learn her how to meddle. And looky here—you drop that school, you hear? I'll learn peo-ple to bring up a boy to put on airs over his own father and let on to be better'n what *he* is. You lemme catch you fooling around that school again, you hear? Your mother couldn't read, and she couldn't write, nuther, before she died. None of the family couldn't before *they* died. *I* can't; and here you're a-swelling yourself up like this, I ain't the man to stand it—you hear? Say, lemme hear you read."

I took up a book and begun something about Gen-eral Washington and the wars. When I'd read about a half a minute, he fetched the book a whack with his hand and knocked it across the house. He says:

"It's so. You can do it. I had my doubts when you told me. Now looky here; you stop that putting on frills. I won't have it. I'll lay for you, my smarty; and if I catch you about that school I'll tan you good. First you know you'll get religion, too. I never see such a son."

He took up a little blue and yaller picture of some cows and a boy, and says:

"What's this?"

"It's something they give me for learning my lessons good."

He tore it up, and says:

"I'll give you something better—I'll give you a cowhide."

He sat there a-mumbling and a-growling a minute, and then he says:

"*Ain't* you a sweet-scented dandy, though? A bed; and bedclothes; and a look'n' glass; and a piece of carpet on the floor—and your own father got to sleep with the hogs in the tanyard. I never see such a son. I bet I'll take some o' these frills out o' you before I'm done with you. Why, there ain't no end to your airs—they say you're rich. Hey?—how's that?"

"They lie—that's how."

"Looky here—mind how you talk to me; I'm a-standing about all I can stand now—so don't gimme no sass. I've been in town two days, and I hain't heard nothing but about you bein' rich. I heard about it away down the river, too. That's why I come. You git me that money tomorrow—I want it."

"I hain't got no money."

"It's a lie. Judge Thatcher's got it. You git it. I want it."

"I hain't got no money, I tell you. You ask Judge Thatcher; he'll tell you the same."

"All right. I'll ask him; and I'll make him pungle, too, or I'll know the reason why. Say, how much you got in your pocket? I want it."

"I hain't got only a dollar, and I want that to—"

"It don't make no difference what you want it for—you just shell it out."

He took it and bit it to see if it was good, and then he said he was going downtown to get some whisky; said he hadn't had a drink all day. When he had got out on the shed he put his head in again, and cussed me for putting on frills and trying to be better than him; and when I reckoned he was gone he came back and put his head in again, and told me to mind about that school, because he was going to lay for me and lick me if I didn't drop that.

Next day he was drunk, and he went to Judge Thatcher's and bullyragged him, and tried to make him give up the money; but he couldn't, and then he swore he'd make the law force him.

The judge and the widow went to law to get the court to take me away from him and let one of them be my guardian; but it was a new judge that had just come, and he didn't know the old man; so he said courts mustn't interfere and separate families if they could help it; said he'd druther not take a child away from its father. So Judge Thatcher and the widow had to quit on the business.

That pleased the old man till he couldn't rest. He said he'd cowhide me till I was black and blue if I didn't raise some money for him. I borrowed three dollars from Judge Thatcher, and pap took it and got drunk, and went a-blowing around and cussing and whooping and carrying on; and he kept it up all over town, with a tin pan, till most midnight; then they jailed him, and the next day they had him before court, and jailed him again for a week. But he said *he* was satisfied; said he was boss of his son, and he'd make it warm for *him*.

When he got out the new judge said he was a-going to make a man of him. So he took him to his own house, and dressed him up clean and nice, and had him to breakfast and dinner and supper with the family, and was just old pie to him, so to speak. And after supper he talked to him about temperance and such things till the old man cried, and said he'd been a fool, and fooled away his life; but now he was a-going to turn over a new leaf and be a man nobody wouldn't be ashamed of, and he hoped the judge would help him and not look down on him. The judge said he could hug him for them words; so *he* cried, and his wife she cried again; pap said he'd been a man that had always been misunderstood before, and the judge said he believed it. The old man said that what a man wanted that was down was sympathy, and the judge said it was so; so they cried again. And when it was bedtime the old man rose up and held out his hand, and says:

"Look at it, gentlemen and ladies all; take a-hold of it; shake it. There's a hand that was the hand of a hog, but it ain't so no more; it's the hand of a man that's started in on a new life, and'll die before he'll go back. You mark them words—don't forget I said them. It's a clean hand now; shake it—don't be afeard."

So they shook it, one after the other, all around, and cried. The judge's wife she kissed it. Then the old man he signed a pledge—made his mark. The judge said it was the holiest time on record, or something like that. Then they tucked the old man into a beautiful room, which was the spare room, and in the night some time he got powerful thirsty and clumb out on to the porch-roof and slid down a stanchion and traded his new coat for a jug of forty-rod, and clumb back again and had a good old time; and toward daylight he crawled out again, drunk as a fiddler, and rolled off the porch and broke his left arm in two places, and was most froze to death when somebody found him after sunup. And when they come to look at that spare room they had to take soundings before they could navigate it.

The judge he felt kind of sore. He said he reckoned a body could reform the old man with a shotgun, maybe, but he didn't know no other way.

Richard Wright

from

Black Boy

It was in this tenement that the personality of my father first came fully into the orbit of my concern. He worked as a night porter in a Beale Street drugstore and he became important and forbidding to me only when I learned that I could not make noise when he was asleep in the daytime. He was the lawgiver in our family and I never laughed in his presence. I used to lurk timidly in the kitchen doorway and watch his huge body sitting slumped at the table. I stared at him with awe as he gulped his beer from a tin bucket, as he ate long and heavily, sighed, belched, closed his eyes to nod on a stuffed belly. He was quite fat and his bloated stomach always lapped over his belt. He was always a stranger to me, always somehow alien and remote.

One morning my brother and I, while playing in the rear of our flat, found a stray kitten that set up a loud, persistent meowing. We fed it some scraps of food and gave it water, but it still meowed. My father, clad in his underwear, stumbled sleepily to the back door and demanded that we keep quiet. We told him that it was the kitten that was making the noise and he ordered us to drive it away. We tried to make the kitten leave, but it would not budge. My father took a hand.

"Scat!" he shouted.

The scrawny kitten lingered, brushing itself against our legs, and meowing plaintively.

"Kill that damn thing!" my father exploded. "Do anything, but get it away from here!"

He went inside, grumbling. I resented his shouting and it irked me that I could never make him feel my resentment. How could I hit back at him? Oh, yes . . . He had said to kill the kitten and I would kill it! I knew that he had not really meant for me to kill the kitten, but my deep hate of him urged me toward a literal acceptance of his word.

"He said for us to kill the kitten," I told my brother.

"He didn't mean it," my brother said.

"He did, and I'm going to kill 'im."

"Then he *will* howl," my brother said.

"He can't howl if he's dead," I said.

"He didn't really say kill 'im," my brother protested.

"He did!" I said. "And you heard him!"

My brother ran away in fright. I found a piece of rope, made a noose, slipped it about the kitten's neck, pulled over a nail, then jerked the animal clear of the ground. It gasped, slobbered, spun, doubled, clawed the air frantically; finally its mouth gaped and its pink-white tongue shot out stiffly. I tied the rope to a nail and went to find my brother. He was crouching behind a corner of the building.

"I killed 'im," I whispered.

"You did bad," my brother said.

"Now Papa can sleep," I said, deeply satisfied.

"He didn't mean for you to kill 'im," my brother said.

"Then why did he *tell* me to do it?" I demanded.

My brother could not answer; he stared fearfully at the dangling kitten.

"That kitten's going to get you," he warned me.

"That kitten can't even breathe now," I said.

"I'm going to tell," my brother said, running into the house.

I waited, resolving to defend myself with my father's rash words, anticipating my enjoyment in repeating them to him even though I knew that he had spoken them in anger. My mother hurried toward me, drying her hands upon her apron. She stopped and paled when she saw the kitten suspended from the rope.

"What in God's name have you done?" she asked.

"The kitten was making noise and Papa said to kill it," I explained.

"You little fool!" she said. "Your father's going to beat you for this!"

"But he told me to kill it," I said.

"You shut your mouth!"

She grabbed my hand and dragged me to my father's bedside and told him what I had done.

"You know better than that!" my father stormed.

"You told me to kill 'im," I said.

"I told you to drive him away," he said.

"You told me to kill 'im," I countered positively.

"You get out of my eyes before I smack you down!" my father bellowed in disgust, then turned over in bed.

I had had my first triumph over my father. I had made him believe that I had taken his words literally. He could not punish me now without risking his authority. I was happy because I had at last found a way to throw my criticism of him into his face. I had made him feel that, if he whipped me for killing the kitten, I would never give serious weight to his words again. I had made him know that I felt he was cruel and I had done it without his punishing me.

WORK

My father . . . had a restaurant, just an ordinary restaurant. It's hard to describe, a family restaurant. I've written about it, but even though I have written about it, I can never remember what the food tasted like, which I suppose basically must be some sort of commentary on the food itself.

At lunch my father wrote poems on the menu, and I always thought that was why he wanted to be in the restaurant business, so he could have an outlet for his poetry. He wrote couplets like "Don't sigh, eat pie." Then he'd rhyme "pie" with lots of things, like "evening is nigh," and "Okay, warden, I'm ready to fry, I've had my last piece of Mrs. Trillin's pie."

CALVIN TRILLIN

My father was always top man on the farm; all the sharecroppers answered to him, and he answered to the owner. Daddy was in charge. TINA TURNER

My father was in the picture business as another man might be in cotton or steel, and I took it tranquilly. BUDD SCHULBERG

My father was the Headmaster of Marlborough Grammar. I would say he was a great man in reduced circumstances. WILLIAM GOLDING

My father was a plumber with his own truck (Adler's Plumbing Shop on Wheels) and I would sometimes go out with him on jobs. Watching as he dug a ditch in which to lay a drainpipe convinced me that, whatever my future, it did not include a career in plumbing. LARRY ADLER

My father played the viola in the Royal Danish Symphony Orchestra. A lot of people don't know the difference between a violin and a viola. Unfortunately, my father was one of them. VICTOR BORGE

My father was a bullshit artist. GEOFFREY WOLFF

That my father is a poet has, at least, saved me from any false reverence for poets. I am even delighted when I meet people who know of him and not of me. I sing some of his songs while washing up after

meals, or shelling peas, or on similar occasions. He
never once tried to teach me how to write, or
showed any understanding of my serious poetry;
being always more ready to ask advice about his
own. Nor did he ever try to stop me writing. His
lighthearted early work is the best. His *Invention of
Wine,* for instance, which begins:

> Ere Bacchus could talk
> Or decently walk,
> Down Olympus he jumped
> From the arms of his nurse,
> And though ten years in all
> Were consumed by the fall
> He might have fallen farther
> And fared a dale worse . . .

After marrying my mother and turning teetotaler,
he is said to have lost something of his playfulness.
ROBERT GRAVES

My dad was the town drunk. Usually that's not so
bad, but New York City?　HENNY YOUNGMAN

My dad was employed as a meteorologist at the
Edgewood Arsenal. They made poison gas there
during world War II, so I guess it would have been
the meteorologist's job to figure out which way the
wind was blowing when it was time to shoot the stuff
off.　FRANK ZAPPA

Dad wanted to be a dentist, and he wound up prac-
ticing in Cleveland. Around Prohibition time. He
was such a sensational dentist, I'm told, that the mob

used to come to him for their mouthwork. My mother worked as his receptionist after they'd been married a while, and she tells me when the gangsters came to get drilled and filled, my dad insisted they check their heat with Mom. There were times, she says, when her desk drawer was difficult to pull open, so filled with guns was it.   HARLAN ELLISON

My father was a small-time dairy farmer in Charlotte, North Carolina. I had to get up at three in the morning and help milk the cows.   BILLY GRAHAM

I didn't know the full facts of life until I was seventeen. My father never talked about his work.
MARTIN FREUD

My father was a [Royal Canadian] Mountie.
LESLIE NIELSEN

My father died in 1973 at the age of ninety-eight. His life span, one-twentieth of the time since Christ, covered the period of the greatest technological change the world has ever known. He was born in 1875 on a 160-acre farm in central Minnesota. He bought cattle in Minnesota, North and South Dakota, and Montana for shipment to the South St. Paul stockyards. He also worked as the postmaster in Watkins until he was ousted by the Democrats after Woodrow Wilson won the 1912 election.
EUGENE McCARTHY

My father was a lodger, visible mainly on Friday evenings, when he brought home a prime joint from

the beef market. For the rest of the time he drank
or tried to cut down on his drinking by playing the
piano in one of the local cinemas. He then combined
both diversions by becoming the regular pianist at
the Golden Eagle, a huge pub on Lodge Street,
Miles Platting.   ANTHONY BURGESS

Art is a business. Artists always thought they were
above it. My father was naive in that sense.
          KATE ROTHKO of her father, Mark Rothko

My father was a man of many trades, but for the
part of his life that I knew him, he was a bookmaker.
Not a crafter of fine volumes, though he allowed my
mother to believe as much while they were courting.
His craft was writing bets on horses and paying off
the winning tickets: white-collar work behind the
counter, he was quick to say.   SHIRLEY ABBOTT

Ever since I can remember, I could turn on the news
and see my father.
               KATHY CRONKITE upon the retirement
               of her father, Walter Cronkite

My father was a lawyer who thought the cornerstone
of culture was the mortgage indenture. He used to
talk about the mortgage indenture at breakfast. He
was a wonderful man.   GEORGE PLIMPTON

My father was a tailor. I used to deliver for him. I'd
have to hold the clothes up high to keep them from
dragging on the ground.   TONY CURTIS

Nineteen seventy-six was ... the year my father died. At his death he left the manuscript of a novel, *The MacGregors,* which was published in 1979. He began to write after he was seventy, after a life of hard work. It was a new kind of hard work and a great wonder and satisfaction to him. He sat up in his hospital bed and wanted to talk of nothing but the development of his characters.   ALICE MUNRO

We grew up completely normal. We didn't even get cars at sixteen, or anything like that. For years I didn't even know what he did. They asked me at school what he did, and I said he was a security analyst, and they thought he checked alarm systems.
   SUSAN BUFFETT of her father, Warren Buffett

My father ... wanted respectability for his family, and for as long as I can remember, he hid behind a facade of legitimacy and tried to keep all his children in the dark about his role in the underworld. Never once did he admit to me or my sisters that he was a mafioso. The closest he ever admitted to being engaged in criminal acts was that he was a gambler. That was it. What he did was "business," and it was none of our business what that business was.   ANTOINETTE GIANCANA

My father ... became rather well known and re-spected for his amazing color photography on Roger Corman and American International Pictures horror films like *The Raven, Tales of Terror, Haunted Palace, The Fall of the House of Usher,* and *The Pit and the Pendulum.* He made twenty-three films with Roger

Corman and later, while I was playing rock 'n' roll on the Sunset Strip for real, my father was filming teen classics like *Bikini Beach, How to Stuff a Wild Bikini,* and *Beach Blanket Bingo.* Talk about a generation gap. It was embarrassing.   DAVID CROSBY

My father was in the Jesuits, in the seminary—before he met my mother.   AIDAN QUINN

My father was a theatrical agent. Growing up in London, our house was filled with jugglers, clowns and actors.   JACKIE COLLINS

He was a strong man doing strong work. Running big freight trains on a single-track railroad in the days of steam locomotives was hard. You started on a steam locomotive as a fireman. You "went to firing." You took a shovel and you held a stance on the gangway between the locomotive and the coal tender, and you shoveled coal, scoop after scoop into the raging firebox. You "fired" the giant engine yourself, with your own hands, your own back and legs, with your own sweat. I've seen firemen come down off steam locomotives with the salt from their bodies showing powder dry on their overalls. Before you got to be promoted to engineer, you fired for years: three years, four years, five.   RED BARBER

He worked stripped to the waist almost the year around, and my most enduring childhood memory of him is seeing him in the ditch, digging, drenched in sweat—sweating as if water were pouring off him—when he first took me along to his job. . . . I was five or six and he wanted to bond with his first-born son. This was his no-nonsense way.

DAN RATHER

He'd had absolutely no training . . . and if you had ever seen one of his suits, you'd realize what an accurate statement that is. You see, Pop never used a tape measure. He didn't believe in it. He said he could just look at a man and tell his size, with the result that frequently he'd make a pair of pants with one trouser leg seven or eight inches longer than the other.

GROUCHO MARX

I never think of myself as a writer. I'm a journalist, a fifth-generation newspaper person. Father was a newspaper editor, a small-town newspaper editor, but he never thought of himself as a writer either. He wrote two thousand words a day for sixty years of his life, but he never used a byline. So when I used a byline, I hid it from my father for years. I was embarrassed by it.

M.F.K. FISHER

My father was, and still is, a barber. He has the curious distinction of having barbered JFK when he was President, and years earlier in the thirties and forties, he used to cut Jack Ruby's hair.

We came to Los Angeles in 1943 from Chicago, where my father had a long and successful "practice." His customers in Chicago were a mixed bag. He had respectable businessmen and he had bookmakers and he had gangsters. When we moved to Los Angeles, for the most part he got a much more refined clientele, but again, he would have Gregory Peck and then perhaps the next customer would be Bugsy Siegel.

When I was sixteen and going to Fairfax High School, one of my father's jobs was to shave Danny Thomas every Sunday. Danny was on the "Fanny Brice Maxwell House Coffee Time" radio show, in which Fanny Brice played a character called "Baby Snooks." She was the star and Danny had a seven- or eight-minute spot on the show called "Jerry Dingle the Postman." It was really Walter Mitty. Each show he would be insulted by someone and Danny would visualize himself in that person's profession and be a much better person for being that person. Anyway, he had this spot every week on the show and my dad used to tidy him up for the studio audience, and somewhere along the line, I don't know what prompted him to do it,—except, not unlike a lot of immigrant parents, he wanted better for me— he told Danny that I was very good at comedy. In fact, I was very good at comedy—but at the high school level. I had done the things you do in high school, especially if you're a showoff. I'd written sketches and monologues for myself and other people, but I never seriously thought that I was going to write comedy for a living. At any rate, Thomas said, "Well, have the kid write something" and so I did, and as a result I was allowed to sit in every day after school with the head writer on the show, Mac Benoff, and that brought me to the attention of an agent named George Gruskin, who was with the William Morris office, and Gruskin said the Morris office would represent me if I wanted to keep doing this. I said I wanted to keep doing this. My dad had to sign the authorization with the agency because I was too young. The first job that they got me was with "Duffy's Tavern," a very popular radio show for a lot of years.

So, my dad acted as a combination Mama Rose and Sweeney Todd—getting me a job at the point of—or along the edge of—a razor.

LARRY GELBART

When you say you're a minister's son, a lot of people immediately imagine this serious, somber parent figure. But my father wasn't like that. He was a funny guy who didn't even have a church. He ran an organization in New York called the New York City Mission Society, a social work agency. He was not a dogmatic person. When I was a kid, we attended the Episcopal church because there was no Presbyterian church in Armonk. My father didn't care. He was one of those guys, when you had a marriage between a Hindu and a Catholic, or a Jew and a Moslem, or two Hindus and a Catholic, or two Hindus, a Catholic and a dog—my father would perform the ceremony. DAVE BARRY

My dad owned a tavern in Appleton, Wisconsin, and when he was behind that bar he was in his glory. He would hold court, dispense advice, philosophize on a variety of subjects. When he sold the place and had to leave that domain, I think he lost something.

ROCKY BLEIER

Kazuo Ishiguro

from

The Remains of
the Day

There was a certain story my father was fond of
repeating over the years. I recall listening to him tell
it to visitors when I was a child, and then later, when
I was starting out as a footman under his supervi-
sion. I remember him relating it again the first time
I returned to see him after gaining my first post as
butler—to a Mr and Mrs Muggeridge in their relatively modest house in Allshot, Oxfordshire. Clearly
the story meant much to him. My father's generation
was not one accustomed to discussing and analysing
in the way ours is, and I believe the telling and re-
telling of this story was as close as my father ever
came to reflecting critically on the profession he
practised. As such, it gives a vital clue to his
thinking.

The story was an apparently true one concerning
a certain butler who had travelled with his employer
to India and served there for many years main-
taining amongst the native staff the same high standards he had commanded in England. One afternoon,

evidently, this butler had entered the dining room to make sure all was well for dinner, when he noticed a tiger languishing beneath the dining table. The butler had left the dining room quietly, taking care to close the doors behind him, and proceeded calmly to the drawing room, where his employer was taking tea with a number of visitors. There he attracted his employer's attention with a polite cough, then whispered in the latter's ear: "I'm very sorry, sir, but there appears to be a tiger in the dining room. Perhaps you will permit the twelve-bores to be used?"

And according to legend, a few minutes later, the employer and his guests heard three gun shots. When the butler reappeared in the drawing room some time afterwards to refresh the teapots, the employer had inquired if all was well.

"Perfectly fine, thank you, sir," had come the reply. "Dinner will be served at the usual time and I am pleased to say there will be no discernible traces left of the recent occurrence by that time."

This last phrase—"no discernible traces left of the recent occurrence by that time"—my father would repeat with a laugh and shake his head admiringly. He neither claimed to know the butler's name, nor anyone who had known him, but he would always insist the event occurred just as he told it. In any case, it is of little importance whether or not this story is true; the significant thing is, of course, what it reveals concerning my father's ideals. For when I look back over his career, I can see with hindsight that he must have striven throughout his years somehow to *become* that butler of his story. And in my view, at the peak of his career, my father achieved his ambition. For although I am sure he never had the chance to encounter a tiger beneath the dining table, when I think over all that I know or have heard concerning him, I can think of at least several instances of his displaying in abundance that very quality he so admired in the butler of his story.

One such instance was related to me by Mr David Charles, of the Charles and Redding Company, who visited Darlington Hall from time to time during Lord Darlington's days. It was one evening when I happened to be valeting him, Mr Charles told me he had come across my father some years earlier while a guest at Loughborough House—the home of Mr John Silvers, the industrialist, where my father served for fifteen years at the height of his career. He had never been quite able to forget my father, Mr Charles told me, owing to an incident that occurred during that visit.

One afternoon, Mr Charles to his shame and regret had allowed himself to become inebriated in the company of two fellow guests—gentlemen I shall merely call Mr Smith and Mr Jones since they are likely to be still remembered in certain circles. After an hour or so of drinking, these two gentlemen decided they wished to go for an afternoon drive around the local villages—a motor car around this time still being something of a novelty. They persuaded Mr Charles to accompany them, and since the chauffeur was on leave at that point, enlisted my father to drive the car.

Once they had set off, Mr Smith and Mr Jones, for all their being well into their middle years, proceeded to behave like schoolboys, singing coarse songs and making even coarser comments on all they saw from the window. Furthermore, these gentlemen had noticed on the local map three villages in the vicinity called Morphy, Saltash and Brigoon. Now I am not entirely sure these were the exact names, but the point was they reminded Mr Smith

and Mr Jones of the music hall act, Murphy, Salt-
man and Brigid the Cat, of which you may have
heard. Upon noticing this curious coincidence, the
gentlemen then gained an ambition to visit the three
villages in question—in honour, as it were, of the
music hall artistes. According to Mr Charles, my father had duly driven to one village and was on the
point of entering a second when either Mr Smith or
Mr Jones noticed the village was Brigoon—that is to
say the third, not the second, name of the sequence.
They demanded angrily that my father turn the car
immediately so that the villages could be visited "in
the correct order." It so happened that this entailed
doubling back a considerable way of the route, but,
so Mr Charles assures me, my father accepted the
request as though it were a perfectly reasonable one,
and in general, continued to behave with immaculate
courtesy.

But Mr Smith's and Mr Jones's attention had now
been drawn to my father and no doubt rather bored
with what the view outside had to offer, they proceeded to amuse themselves by shouting out unflat-
tering remarks concerning my father's "mistake." Mr
Charles remembered marveling at how my father
showed not one hint of discomfort or anger, but
continued to drive with an expression balanced perfectly between personal dignity and readiness to
oblige. My father's equanimity was not, however, allowed to last. For when they had wearied of hurling
insults at my father's back, the two gentlemen began
to discuss their host—that is to say, my father's employer, Mr John Silvers. The remarks grew ever
more debased and treacherous so that Mr Charles—
at least so he claimed—was obliged to intervene with
the suggestion that such talk was bad form. This
view was contradicted with such energy that Mr

Charles, quite aside from worrying whether he would become the next focus of the gentlemen's attention, actually thought himself in danger of physical assault. But then suddenly, following a particularly heinous insinuation against his employer, my father brought the car to an abrupt halt. It was what happened next that had made such an indelible impression upon Mr Charles.

The rear door of the car opened and my father was observed to be standing there, a few steps back from the vehicle, gazing steadily into the interior. As Mr Charles described it, all three passengers seemed to be overcome as one by the realization of what an imposing physical force my father was. Indeed, he was a man of some six feet three inches, and his countenance, though reassuring while one knew he was intent on obliging, could seem extremely forbidding viewed in certain other contexts. According to Mr Charles, my father did not display any obvious anger. He had, it seemed, merely opened the door. And yet there was something so powerfully rebuking and at the same time so unassailable about his figure looming over them that Mr Charles's two drunken companions seemed to cower back like small boys caught by the farmer in the act of stealing apples.

My father had proceeded to stand there for some moments, saying nothing, merely holding open the door. Eventually, either Mr Smith or Mr Jones had remarked: "Are we not going on with the journey?"

My father did not reply, but continued to stand there silently, neither demanding disembarkation nor offering any clue as to his desires or intentions. I can well imagine how he must have looked that day, framed by the doorway of the vehicle, his dark, severe presence quite blotting out the effect of the gentle Hertfordshire scenery behind him. Those were, Mr Charles recalls, strangely unnerving moments during which he too, despite not having participated in the preceding behavior, felt engulfed with guilt. The silence seemed to go on interminably, before either Mr Smith or Mr Jones found it in him to mutter: "I suppose we were talking a little out of turn there. It won't happen again."

A moment to consider this, then my father had closed the door gently, returned to the wheel and had proceeded to continue the tour of the three villages—a tour, Mr Charles assured me, that was completed thereafter in near-silence.

Now that I have recalled this episode, another event from around that time in my father's career comes to mind which demonstrates perhaps even more impressively this special quality he came to possess. I should explain here that I am one of two brothers—and that my elder brother, Leonard, was killed during the Southern African War while I was still a boy. Naturally, my father would have felt this loss keenly; but to make matters worse, the usual comfort a father has in these situations—that is, the notion that his son gave his life gloriously for king and country—was sullied by the fact that my brother had perished in a particularly infamous manoeuvre. Not only was it alleged that the manoeuvre had been a most un-British attack on civilian Boer settlements, overwhelming evidence emerged that it had been irresponsibly commanded with several floutings of elementary military precautions, so that the men who had died—my brother among them—had died quite needlessly. In view of what I am about to relate, it would not be proper of me to identify the manoeuvre any more precisely, though you may well guess which one I am alluding to if I say that it caused something of an uproar at the time, adding

significantly to the controversy the conflict as a
whole was attracting. There had been calls for the
removal, even the court-martialling, of the general
concerned, but the army had defended the latter
and he had been allowed to complete the campaign.
What is less known is that at the close of the Southern African conflict, this same general had been dis-
creetly retired, and he had then entered business,
dealing in shipments from Southern Africa. I relate
this because some ten years after the conflict, that is
to say when the wounds of bereavement had only
superficially healed, my father was called into Mr
John Silvers's study to be told that this very same
personage—I will call him simply "the General"—
was due to visit for a number of days to attend a
house party, during which my father's employer
hoped to lay the foundations of a lucrative business
transaction. Mr Silvers, however, had remembered
the significance the visit would have for my father,
and had thus called him in to offer him the option
of taking several days' leave for the duration of the
General's stay.

My father's feelings towards the General were,
naturally, those of utmost loathing; but he realized
too that his employer's present business aspirations
hung on the smooth running of the house party—
which with some eighteen or so people expected
would be no trifling affair. My father thus replied
to the effect that while he was most grateful that his
feelings had been taken into account, Mr Silvers
could be assured that service would be provided to
the usual standards.

As things turned out, my father's ordeal proved
even worse than might have been predicted. For one
thing, any hopes my father may have had that to
meet the General in person would arouse a sense of

respect or sympathy to leaven his feelings against him proved without foundation. The General was a portly, ugly man, his manners were not refined, and his talk was conspicuous for an eagerness to apply military similes to a very wide variety of matters. Worse was to come with the news that the gentleman had brought no valet, his usual man having fallen ill. This presented a delicate problem, another of the house guests being also without his valet, raising the question as to which guest should be allocated the butler as valet and who the footman. My father, appreciating his employer's position, volunteered immediately to take the General, and thus was obliged to suffer intimate proximity for four days with the man he detested. Meanwhile, the General, having no idea of my father's feelings, took full opportunity to relate anecdotes of his military accomplishments—as of course many military gentlemen are wont to do to their valets in the privacy of their rooms. Yet so well did my father hide his feelings, so professionally did he carry out his duties, that on his departure the General had actually complimented Mr John Silvers on the excellence of his butler and had left an unusually large tip in appreciation—which my father without hesitation asked his employer to donate to a charity.

I hope you will agree that in these two instances I have cited from his career—both of which I have had corroborated and believe to be accurate—my father not only manifests, but comes close to being the personification itself, of what the Hayes Society terms "dignity in keeping with his position." If one considers the difference between my father at such moments and a figure such as Mr Jack Neighbours even with the best of his technical flourishes, I believe one may begin to distinguish what it is that separates a "great" butler from a merely competent one. We may now understand better, too, why my father was so fond of the story of the butler who failed to panic on discovering a tiger under the dining table; it was because he knew instinctively that somewhere in this story lay the kernel of what true "dignity" is.

FATHERLY
ADVICE

Look thou character. Give thy thoughts no tongue,
Nor any unproportioned thought his act.
Be thou familiar, but by no means vulgar.
Those friends thou hast, and their adoption tried,
Grapple them unto thy soul with hoops of steel.
But do not dull thy palm with entertainment
Of each new-hatched, unfledged courage. Beware
Of entrance to a quarrel. But, being in,
Bear't that th' opposed may beware of thee.
Give every man thine ear, but few thy voice.
Take each man's censure, but reserve thy judgment.
Costly thy habit as thy purse can buy,
But not expressed in fancy; rich, not gaudy;
For the apparel oft proclaims the man,
And they in France of the best rank and station
Are of a most select and generous chief in that.
Neither a borrower nor a lender be,
For loan oft loses both itself and friend,
And borrowing dulleth edge of husbandry.
This above all: to thine own self be true,

And it must follow, as the night the day,
Thou canst not then be false to any man.
POLONIUS to his son, Laertes, in *Hamlet*, Act I, Scene 3

Never get sick, Hubert, there isn't time.
HUBERT H. HUMPHREY's father

Always go with people who are smarter than you
are—and in your case it won't be difficult.
FRANCIS CARDINAL SPELLMAN's father

Never have partners.   HOWARD HUGHES's father

If a man starts a sentence with the word *frankly,* you
know he's going to lie to you.
STEWART ALSOP's father

My dad told me there's no difference between a
black snake and a white snake. They both bite.
THURGOOD MARSHALL

On my twenty-first birthday my father said, "Son,
here's a million dollars. Don't lose it."
LARRY NIVEN

Be perfectly natural with people of high rank, but
with everyone else please behave like an Englishman.
WOLFGANG AMADEUS MOZART's father

"If you don't open your mouth, Aissa, then you can't get in trouble," he told me repeatedly throughout my childhood and, without fail, prior to any meeting with the press. "The only way to get in trouble, the only way for people to think you're a jerk, is if you open your mouth."

AISSA WAYNE's father, John Wayne

My father, author of religious books, was in his own fashion a "literateur." Since I was curious about what he wrote, Father confided his views to me. He had his favorites among the commentaries, and those which he considered incomprehensible. Assuming that when I grew up I too would write religious books, he gave me the following advice. "Be straightforward in your reasoning and avoid casuistry. None of the great scholars tortured the text. True, they dug deeply, but they never made mountains out of molehills."

ISAAC BASHEVIS SINGER

My father, who was Roman Catholic, had been through the First World War, and when *my* war started, he took me off to the train station and said, "Just remember one thing, sweetheart: He doesn't keep His eye on the sparrows. He's too busy with other things. So don't be a sparrow."

DIRK BOGARDE

"You don't have to wave at the waiter like that to get his attention, lad," Dad told me over dinner at

Romanoff's. "Watch." He merely arched his eyebrow, and the waiter appeared instantly. Then it was my turn. I spent the rest of the meal trying to catch the waiter's eye. I'll bet everyone else there felt sorry Yul's kid had such a terrible twitch.

ROCK BRYNNER of his father, Yul Brynner

Father was never late. Indeed, punctuality was his eleventh commandment. He saw lateness as a signal to the boss that you didn't care about your job, a potentially suicidal misstep. "If you're to be there at seven," he lectured me, "you be there at six forty-five. And you don't go to the water bucket more than once an hour."

DAN RATHER

The little Dad owned he took care of. He had a farmer's respect for tools. He kept his pocketknife sharp. He edged it on an oilstone, careful of the angle. He carried his watch on a leather fob in a watch pocket at his waist and dangled it at my ear when I asked him to let me hear it tick; he wound it formally once a day, springing open the case to check the time and snapping it shut. He always had the correct time; he set his watch by a railroad chronometer at work. He polished his own shoes and taught us to polish ours. One of his belts was carefully stitched together in back where it had broken. Good shoes and belts, he'd tell us, would last fifteen years.

RICHARD RHODES

If you see something and you know it isn't yours—don't pick it up.

RED BARBER's father

Dear Kath,

Can't let your twenty-first birthday go by without a wee bit of sentimental indulgence. You are now a free lance and your dad has no control over you. Just think of that! Doesn't it make you shudder when you think of the past twenty-one years of servitude. Just for that I now shall order you around as successfully in the future as in the past.

First, don't take life or its happenings too seriously. Lift up the corners of that mouth that I gave you one moonlit night.

Second, try to do one thing well—utilizing the experience of all preceding life and your own wit.

Third, never let yourself *hate* any person. It is the most devastating weapon of one's enemies.

Fourth, always remember that your dad is liable to call you all sorts of names when he disapproves of your behavior, but don't take him too seriously, and always come to him—whatever your difficulty—he may be able to help you. Impossibly, he may not be as stupid as he looks.

Fifth, forget all the above and remember only that I would love to kiss you twenty-one times and give you a million dollars—

Your hopeless Dad
KATHARINE HEPBURN's father

Dad told all the boys to get laid as often as possible.
JOHN F. KENNEDY

My old man lived to be ninety-six and he was drunk for the last fifty years of his life and smoked fifteen cigars a day. He used to say, "Nothing in moderation!"
ALAN KING

My dad always used to say, "Only stupid people play football." My dad was right.   AHMAD RASHAD

I've always had the feeling I could do anything; my daddy told me I could, and I was in college before I found out he might be wrong.   ANN RICHARDS

My father taught me how to deal with overly male men: don't react, just say yes and don't pay any attention.   KATHARINE HEPBURN

My father was tolerant of priests, doubtful of all politicians, generally suspicious of doctors, and slow to take pride in sons or daughters. He was wary of seed dealers and farm organizers. "Watch out for farmers," he would say, "who put signs at their gates or let people paint ads on their barns that read, 'Member of Farmers' Organization' or 'De Laval Cream Separator Used Here.' The next sign you'll see here will be 'Farm for Sale.'" As we drove through the countryside, he would observe, "You can tell a German's farm from an Irishman's. The Germans start with a big barn and a small house. The big house comes later. The Irish start with a large house and a small barn. Neither is ever changed."   EUGENE MCCARTHY

Groucho used to say, "Beware of couples who hold hands." And then he'd quote the old vaudeville joke: "They hold hands because they're afraid if they let go they'll kill each other."   ARTHUR MARX

I had heard my father say that he never knew a piece of land [to] run away or break. JOHN ADAMS

My prescription for success is based on something my father always used to tell me: you should never try to be better than someone else, but you should never cease trying to be the best that you can be.
JOHN WOODEN

He was opposed to the taking of oaths. Not only did he object to oaths, he objected even to pledges, words of honor, or handshaking as guarantees for the fulfillment of a promise. One can never fully trust one's own memory, Father argued; therefore, one must not swear even to what one believes to be the truth. ISAAC BASHEVIS SINGER

My ex-husband was a TV addict. He kept them going day and night because he liked the noise. After I left him, I never wanted to be in the presence of another set, so when I moved into my own apartment I didn't buy one. When my father discovered this he looked at me with great sadness and said, "You know, it's really killing me, the thought of you living alone without a television." I assured him it was okay, but Dad said, "No, it really makes me worry to think that you're all alone without a television set." He handed me a check and said, "I want you to do me a personal favor. I want you to go out and I want you to get yourself a television set. A color television. With a remote control."

When I protested that I didn't need or want a set he became even more insistent: "It doesn't matter. I'll sleep easier at night knowing that you have a television." So I went to one of those discount places where they have walls of televisions going all at once and I immediately had a panic attack because it reminded me of my marriage. I couldn't buy a set; I ran out of the store. But my father was relentless: he kept calling asking if I'd bought my television, so I had to overcome my fear.

I finally got a friend to go back to the store with me and we eventually found a set that didn't remind me of my ex-husband. When they delivered it to my apartment I had them put it in the closet without opening the carton. When Dad called I assured him that I now owned a set and he rested easy.

One day, several years later, after I had moved back to L.A., the man I was dating was at my apartment and he asked why I didn't have a TV. When I showed him the one in the closet he was amazed: "You've got a twenty-six-inch Trinitron that's never been opened." I told him he could hook it up if he liked. He was thrilled. We got married a short time later.

I guess my father was right.   MARGO KAUFMAN

Colin McEnroe

Faerieland

Late one Friday afternoon in the thick of July 1976, my father went walking into the hot breath of the Connecticut summer and, as they say, overdid it.

His doctor had told him to take long walks and neglected to add "but not in the atmospheric equivalent of a vaporizer." So he set out in a purposeful stride and ambled along until his faculties began to veer out of whack.

When he got home, he was dizzy and disoriented. There wasn't anything terribly wrong with him. His body had simply decided that his brain couldn't be trusted and relieved it of command. When I arrived on the scene forty-five minutes later, he had improved to a state of cognitive bleariness, which is, among adult male McEnroes, what passes for normal.

I was twenty-two. I needed at that moment to jump in my Mercury Capri 2000 (a figure that, coincidentally, approximated the number of mechanical liabilities in that car) and drive from Connecticut to

Virginia to see a woman. My mother, for a welter of reasons, didn't want me to go.

"Your father is not well," she told me.

"Go. I'm fine," my father murmured in a cloudy voice. "I was influenced momentarily by elves."

"He's joking now, but half an hour ago, he didn't even know who he was," my mother said.

My father gazed off into the middle distance, as if weighing this statement. Then he looked back into the room and smiled beatifically.

"My name is Claude Rains," he said. "I am a movie actor."

I left.

But this is my favorite Robert E. McEnroe story, because in it he is funny, infuriating, knowing, foolish.

In other words, the consummate Irishman.

I like the story too, because it catches my father looking, as he always does from time to time, into faerieland.

My father once wrote a play about leprechauns. A producer showed it to the eminent British actor Sir Cedric Hardwicke. Hardwicke wanted nothing to do with it, because "it's about faeries and Englishmen don't believe in faeries."

Irishmen do. A gentle acquaintance with faeries makes certain troubles—including Englishmen—a lighter burden.

Not that troubles ever grow so light as to fly away for good.

My father's father lived in New Britain, Connecticut, and owned bars. He fell in love with a woman who was lace curtain Irish, but she wouldn't marry him unless he got out of the gin mill business, which was incorrigibly shanty Irish stuff. He obliged, got into real estate and made a bundle. He learned the real estate game from a man named Smiley Tatum, which may account, my father says, for his lack of conservative thinking. He was a millionaire, living in Florida with his wife and only child, when the crash came in '29 and wiped him out. Mrs. McEnroe walked out on them. My grandfather took young Bob (around twelve or thirteen by my count) and went in search of his wife. I believe they caught up to her in Washington, D.C. Things get a little foggy right around here, but young Bob wound up with his mother, back in Hartford.

That's as much of the story as I know, and it took thirty-five years to get it, mostly secondhand. It explains a lot. My father is a handsome man, in a Spencer Tracy way, rough face, hawkish nose, thick body. In all the old pictures, though, there's a wild look buried in his eyes—like a wolf pretending to be tame but ready to bolt for the woods the day someone gets careless with the cage door.

When he wasn't writing plays, my father worked as a real estate agent. For a while, he toiled in an office where each phone had a row of buttons that would light up as the lines were engaged. The last button in the row would occasionally light up out of sequence, a sign (my father divined) that someone was trying to call the Harte Volkswagen dealership and had misdialed.

My father made a point of being the one to answer those calls.

"Ja," he would begin. And then, in a perfectly dreadful German accent: "Dis is der Black Forest Volkswagen company."

"Oh. I'm not sure I have the right number."

"Ja," my father would say. And then he would go on at some length about the little elves in the Black

Forest, how they make the Volkswagens with great care and pride in their magic.

Then he would try to sell the caller a Volkswagen kit for $750. He would dilate upon the money-saving advantages, the easy-to-read instructions, his willingness to loan them the tools, and of course the everlasting gratitude of the elves.

He never sold one of these kits, partly because it would come out during his spiel that the instructions, although easy to read, were in German. But I suspect he occasionally crossed a line and started to halfway believe he had a kit to sell.

Boundaries have never been his strong point. When I was five, my best friend Ruthie Sapherstein told me there was no Santa Claus. My father overheard it and told her—in a spirit of genial nihilism— that Moses was a fake. Irving and Bunny Sapherstein were not amused.

There. Now you've met him.

My parents are cleaning out their possessions. The other day, when I was picking up my son, my mother shoved an armload of papers at me. It was a lot of embarrassing stuff from my childhood, but one big envelope contained a batch of letters to my father. Most of them go something like this.

Dear Mr. McEnroe you are Writing a good play. your work in a Room. I bet your work is heard is it? I bet colin likes you very much! you are nice. Are your fimly haPPy? I think They are very HaPPy Who are the people inthe play? love Christine Laski.

The letters are from my first grade class. It was the spring of 1961, and *Donnybrook,* a musical comedy with book by Robert E. McEnroe, was opening on Broadway. It was my father's second Broadway show.

Wait a minute.

Was our fimly haPPy? I say yes. Unhappy child-
hoods have become so fashionable nowadays that it's
tempting to insist I had one. It's all in how you stack
the memory blocks, of course. My childhood was
sometimes odd and frequently rather lonely, but my
mother and father loved me and cared for me, their
only issue. I am not an adult child of anything nor
do I have an inner child mewling away inside me.

The only burden peculiar to my life was watching
my father's falling out with his faeries.

You see, *Donnybrook*, his second Broadway show,
was also his last. His first, *The Silver Whistle*, was a
gigantic hit in the late 1940s.

An obligatory stint in Hollywood followed. Then
Donnybrook. His next script would attract a lot of op-
tions, but they all fizzled out. The script after that
would be optioned so many times, we all lost count.
There were some preliminary readings and talks
with a director (Burgess Meredith, I think). Then it
fizzled out too.

Then the writing got hard. When I talk to other
writers about going to faerieland, they always know
exactly what I mean—the place you go where you
find all the things that other people think you make
up. You can't go there if the faeries won't take you,
and they don't like back seat drivers. It's always a
fragile alliance. I believe my father may have quar-
reled with them just a little, and they became less
willing to lead him where he wanted to go.

I'd come downstairs in the morning and peer at
the words scratched in the sharp black lightning of
my father's handwriting. Any progress? Was it a
good play? I bet this work is h(e)ard, is it?

In May of 1961, I didn't know to worry about all
that. My father was a writer. So, I told anyone who

asked, would I be. I remember the letter-writing day in class well enough, because I was in dutch with the teacher for daydreaming, a lifelong vice. As everyone worked on missives to my father, I was finishing up some exercise I hadn't brought in on deadline. In fact, my memory tells me I never got to write one of those letters, but memory is often wrong. Look:

Dear Dadde, Donnybrook was nice when the Champion came to Ireland.

Not in the Christine Laski category, but what do you want? I was under a lot of pressure.

That same year, my mother and I drove to New York City to watch a dress rehearsal of *Donnybrook*. It was common, in those days, to rehearse in a theater on the Bowery, which was even then a very bad part of the city. We parked on the street, and I looked around. The area teemed with bums, as they were then called. A child of the Connecticut suburbs, I had never seen bums.

When we came back from the show, a bum was urinating on the side of my mother's car.

My mother must have guessed at the impression this made on me, because three years later, after an especially mediocre fourth grade report card, she informed me that I was on a daydreamy, lackadaisical track toward degeneracy. If I persisted, I would eventually join the incontinent throng of my brothers in the Bowery.

That did it. I launched myself on a preposterous zoom to the top of my class. When my zeal flagged, there would come, unbidden, the image of me, dirty, ragged, shuffling, unzipping next to green Pontiac. Onward.

As for the writing life, by the time I reached junior high school I had decided: Let this cup pass from me.

I would forge for myself a career based on certainty and reliability, not a bunch of goddamned elves. I would go to sleep every night and wake up in the morning confident that I could do my job and earn a handsome living.

I would be a lawyer.

This was no idle fancy. By ninth grade, I had fallen into the habit of spending school vacation days at the courthouse. Put on a tie, catch the bus, head downtown.

I didn't require James M. Cain material—sex-mad lovers and butcher knives. Nope. A run-of-the-bench liability case would suit me fine. I watched a trial in which the plaintiff had injured himself opening a defective soda bottle. Could the plaintiff have contributed to his own woes by opening the bottle in some inventive manner that did not conform to the laws of healthy human understanding? What were those laws? There were hours of testimony and actual demonstrations of proper church-key technique.

Lord, how I tried to persuade myself this was interesting. I wasn't a good enough lawyer to win that case. The soda bottle could never be anything but a soda bottle, and the witnesses would never be anybody except who they were. The best advocates had an imaginative flair, but they kept their eyes on the ball. I daydreamed. Would you want a lawyer who had one foot in faerieland?

Ah, yes, the faeries. They beckoned. They sang in my ear. I went kicking and screaming, but I was my father's son after all. I wrote, I invented, I dreamed on paper. My mind wouldn't stay in one place. I was useless for almost anything except writing.

*   *   *

The rest of this story is about writing—which is always a dull story. I wrote. He wrote.

Nothing I ever wrote was ever as wondrous as my father's work in full flower, but I was happy about that. The faeries were only giving me the fifty-cent tour, so I had less to lose when they pulled out.

Which I was sure they would do. On my second date with the woman who is now my wife, I explained calmly and seriously that, in the interests of full disclosure, she should know that somewhere down the road I would become a derelict and urinate on cars.

Meanwhile, even as I erected this sorrowful legend of myself, my father, year by year, hammered out a new treaty with faerieland.

When he couldn't get anything published or produced, my father would write simply to amuse the people in his real estate offices. Some archivist should collect all that stuff. I remember a pie company he invented and named after an actual local Revolutionary War heroine. Sarah Whitman Hooker Pies—"Try a Hooker for a change!" For several weeks, he issued brochures and ad copy for such confections as Colonel Elwood's Sensible Peach for Young Christian Women.

As with the Black Forest Volkswagens, he acted as though these pies might actually exist somewhere.

One day last year, I was on the phone with Robert E. McEnroe, who is seventy-six and has back trouble, which makes it difficult for him to walk.

"Your mother and the doctors are talking about surgery with great relish," he said in an amused way. "The message I'm getting is that I better learn to walk again pretty goddamned quick."

When I hung up, I smiled at my wife, whose father died three days after Christmas, 1990.

"I don't know how much longer we'll have him," she said in a soft way. "So we should enjoy Bob McEnroe while we can."

Enjoy. Now there's an idea. In thirty-seven years I have loved him, strained against him, worried about him and worried even more about me.

But it seems like years since I have remembered to do what most people do with Robert E. McEnroe. Enjoy him. Watch his slow, strange dance with the faeries and relish his peculiar reports back from that world.

It seems that everywhere I go, some days, people leap up from desks and say, "How's your father? Is he writing anything? Do you know what he told me one time?"

And now there's yet another little boy in the story too. My son, Joey, adopted, Mexican-American. He is two and a half. He's been blasting into the room as I've written this, pointing at the letters on the screen, demanding to know what the hell I'm doing. Writing, I say. About Bob. Joey worships Bob. Bob is his shaman. Nobody had to tell Joey that Bob sees faeries.

One day, about a year ago, I came upon Bob and Joey, who was racing around my parents' apartment, misplacing things. My father was holding up a cassette and saying to Joey, in a perfectly adult voice, "Mr. Dwarf. Do you remember where you put the box that this goes in?"

So Joey is apparently quite welcome in the other universe.

Every once in a while, writing a piece like this, you wise up.

So yesterday, I got up from this desk and drove to the newspaper, taking a long cut by the park where I knew they'd all be.

I didn't stop. I just spied on them as I drove past the duck pond. There was my mother, my wife, my little boy. And standing off to the side was a man, ruddy faced, a little stooped, with hair as white as a polar bear's. He was breaking off pieces of bread and tossing them gently forward into the warm air of a spring morning. It may have been a trick of the landscape, but I didn't see any ducks.

LEGACIES

I cannot remember having ever heard a single sentence uttered by my mother in the nature of moral or religious instruction. My father made an effort or two. When he caught me imitating him by pretending to smoke a toy pipe he advised me very earnestly never to follow his example in any way; and his sincerity so impressed me that to this day I have never smoked, never shaved, and never used alcoholic stimulants. He taught me to regard him as an unsuccessful man with many undesirable habits, as a warning and not as a model. In fact, he did himself some injustice lest I should grow up like him; and I now see that this anxiety on his part was admirable and lovable; and that he was really just what he so carefully strove not to be: that is, a model father.   GEORGE BERNARD SHAW

My father was fond of me, & used to take me on his knee, and hold long conversations with me. I

174

remember, that at eight years old I walked with him one winter evening from a farmer's house, a mile from Ottery—& he told me the names of the stars— and how Jupiter was a thousand times larger than our world—and that the other twinkling stars were Suns that had worlds rolling round them—& when I came home, he showed me how they rolled round ... I heard him with a profound delight & admiration; but without the least mixture of wonder or incredulity. For from my early reading of Faery Tales, & Genii &c &c—my mind had been habituated *to the Vast.*   SAMUEL TAYLOR COLERIDGE

Life had given my father a beating, beginning with his hard childhood peddling papers in Trenton; his own father's failures and sorrow and early death had poured through him like rain through a broken window. And his, in turn, through me: the beating showed on his face, in the battered nose repeatedly broken by playing college football, in his sunken triangular eyes; it showed in the gallows humor of his talk, in his pathetic sweat-stained truss and repeatedly aggravated hernia, in the varicose veins on his milk-white legs.   JOHN UPDIKE

While my mother was the dominant presence and had enormous energy for working and was very affectionate and strongly opinionated and easily hurt and very alive in her family presence, all the same, she didn't dominate my father. She overpowered nine out of ten arguments, but he'd wait and win the biggest one. He waited. And my sister and I were never afraid of her. I was always a little afraid of my father. He was extraordinarily private and had an element of the deeply unpredictable about him, and I'm very grateful to him for that because if he hadn't I would have had a totally distorted view of the power of women over men.

NORMAN MAILER

He was very literary. He loved poetry, he loved Shakespeare, he loved Browning. And he was a great barrister. He was a wonderful cross-examiner. And he was very eccentric in many ways: He had the most terrible temper. It used to shatter people. You're going to be very polite to solicitors who bring you work, but he used to shout things at them like, "The devil damn thee black, thou cream-faced loon!"—to teach them Shakespeare. He was extraordinary. But he was very nice to me and always treated me as though I was grown up from a very early age. And then he went blind in the middle of his life. He took no notice of that really: He continued to stand up in court and fix witnesses with his clear blue eyes. But because he was blind I used to read to him, and so I got to know a lot of poetry, and that was very good for me. I read aloud to him a lot. Then when we ran out of things to read I started to write and he would listen to it and tell me whether it was good or not. And he was always right about that. So I still think of whether he would like what I'm writing. He's become a sort of standard for me.

JOHN MORTIMER

I believe that my father's Jewishness profoundly shaped my own identity, and our family existence. They were shaped both by external anti-Semitism and my father's self-hatred, and by his Jewish pride. What Arnold did, I think, was call his Jewish pride something else: achievement, aspiration, genius, idealism. Whatever was unacceptable got left back under the rubric of Jewishness, or the "wrong kind" of Jews: uneducated, aggressive, loud. The message I got was that we were really superior: nobody else's father had collected so many books, had traveled so far, knew so many languages. Baltimore was a musical city, but for the most part, in the families of my school friends, culture was for women. My father was an amateur musician, read poetry, adored encyclopedic knowledge. He prowled and pounced over my school papers, insisting I use "grown up" sources; he criticized my poems for faulty technique and gave me books on rhyme and meter and form. His investment in my intellect and talent was egotistical, tyrannical, opinionated and terribly wearing. He taught me nevertheless to believe in hard work, to mistrust easy inspiration, to write and rewrite; to feel that I *was* the person of the book, even though a woman; to take ideas seriously. He made me feel, at a very young age, the power of language, and that I could share in it.   ADRIENNE RICH

My father was an honorable man. The trouble with being the son of an honorable man is that you constantly feel that you are not living up to the standards he bequeathed you. But once you've learned how to deal with that, you're better off.

                                    FRANK DEFORD

My father never kept a diary, but he never threw away a cancelled check, either. When he died a few years ago I came across thousands of them in perfect order in a series of shoeboxes. Amid stacks of others that took the family from the children's milk through his own bifocals, I found the one that paid the doctor who delivered me. My father knew they didn't audit you for 1951 in 1980; he kept those checks for another reason.   · THOMAS MALLON

After he died, my mother found an old checkbook among his effects, and the stubs read as high as $150 and $200, all to his bookmaker. That money would have seemed a fortune to us if we had seen even half of it.   JAMES CAGNEY

My father won some money in a horse race and managed to send me to journalism school at the University of Texas.   LIZ SMITH

When I was quite small, my wealthy grandfather left my sister and me quite a sum of money, but we never received a penny of it. My father had been made trustee of our inheritance and he spent the lot. I didn't mind; he was such fun, I'd have given him anything.   HERMIONE GINGOLD

Dad was a kind of country philosopher who had almost gotten his degree in philosophy at Johns Hopkins University. He loved to speculate on philosophical meaning. I guess I inherited the same trait.   SHIRLEY MACLAINE

My father was frightened of his father, I was frightened of my father, and I am damned well going to see to it that my children are frightened of me.

KING GEORGE V

My father was truly delighted with my enthusiasm for physics experiments and mathematical problems, and it was taken for granted that I would study physics at the university. Perhaps one element in this was his hope that I would achieve more than he had been able to. But far more important to him was his desire that I find satisfaction and fulfillment in my work. He was constantly warning me against any form of snobbery. He passed on to his children his own firm conviction that work done conscientiously, professionally, and with zest is work well done.

ANDREI SAKHAROV

I like to believe I've inherited some of my father's talent at teaching. It's crucial for me in my television role not to come across as preaching, much less hectoring. I do think of myself not only as a deliverer of news but as an explainer, which I suppose is pretty close to being a teacher.   DAN RATHER

He had an excellent Constitution of Body, was of middle Stature, but well set and very strong. He was ingenious, could draw prettily, was skill'd a little in Music and had a clear pleasing Voice, so that when he play'd Psalm Tunes on his Violin & sung withal as he sometimes did in an Evening after the Business of the Day was over, it was extremely agreeable to hear. He had a mechanical Genius too, and on occa-

sion was very handy in the Use of other Trades-
men's Tools. But his great Excellence lay in a sound
Understanding, and solid Judgment in prudential
Matters, both in private & public Affairs. . . . At his
Table he lik'd to have as often as he could, some
sensible Friend or Neighbor, to converse with, and
always took care to start some ingenious or useful
Topic for Discourse, which might tend to improve
the Minds of his Children. By this means he turn'd
our Attention to what was good, just, & prudent in
the Conduct of Life; and little or no Notice was ever
taken of what related to the Victuals on the Table,
whether it was well or ill dressed, in or out of season,
of good or bad flavor, preferable or inferior to this
or that other thing of the kind; so that I was bro't
up in such a perfect Inattention to those Matters as
to be quite Indifferent to what kind of Food was set
before me; and so unobservant of it, that to this Day,
if I am ask'd I can scarce tell, a few Hours after
Dinner, what I din'd upon. This has been a Conve-
nience to me in travelling, where my Companions
have been sometimes very unhappy for want of a
suitable Gratification of their more delicate because
better instructed tastes and appetites.

BENJAMIN FRANKLIN of his father, Josiah Franklin

My father was wonderfully talented. From him I inherited my memory, my intuition for creative solu-
tions in difficult situations, my love for stability,
precision and harmony. . . . [I saw my first chess
game] on my father's knees.   ANATOLY KARPOV

I was president of Fox when I was twenty-two years
old because my father gave me the studio as a birthday present.   RICHARD ZANUCK

I inherited a somewhat cranky point of view on education from my father. He was really against primary education altogether because he thought kids should learn directly from life as long as they could. That was partly because his father had the same theory and didn't send *my* father to school until he was ten years old or so. WILFRID SHEED

My father was a big, six-foot-four, very black man. He had only one eye. How he lost the other eye I have never known. He was from Reynolds, Georgia, where he had left school after the third or maybe fourth grade. He believed, as did Marcus Garvey, that freedom, independence and self-respect could never be achieved by the Negro in America, and that therefore the Negro should leave America to the white man and return to his African land of origin. Among the reasons my father had decided to risk and dedicate his life to help disseminate this philosophy among his people was that he had seen four of his six brothers die by violence, three of them killed by white men, including one by lynching. What my father could not know then was that of the remaining three, including himself, only one, my Uncle Jim, would die in bed, of natural causes. Northern white police were later to shoot my Uncle Oscar. And my father was finally himself to die by the white man's hands.

It has always been my belief that I, too, will die by violence. MALCOLM X

Of course my father was a great influence on me. He taught me how to read. MICHAEL FOOT

My father was a very good amateur pianist. One of my earliest memories was of sitting under the piano while my father played through the standard German repertoire, Beethoven, Brahms, Schubert. We always had chamber music in the house. All the great symphonies are arranged in Germany for four hands, and my father and I used to sit down at the piano and play them together. He insisted on my being able to sight-read. Of course we made mistakes all the time, but we got through them.

ANDRÉ PREVIN

My father was an intellectual and our home was filled with talk.   HARRY GOLDEN

My father . . . used to bounce me on his knee when I was five years old and say, "Movies, movies, movies." So obviously something sank in.

NATASHA RICHARDSON of her father,
Tony Richardson

He was a coach until he was fired, and then he was a salesman. He had been an All-High quarterback, despite being a little guy, and we would play baseball together and we went to games, primarily the Cleveland Indians. And he was also a referee. He officiated football, basketball, and track meets, and he took me with him whenever he could. When we'd go to games as spectators he was always on the offi-

cial's side. People would scream at the referee and
he'd turn around and say, "Shut up! You don't know
what you're talking about. The ref's a lot closer than
you." Ever since I've always tried to see the official's
point of view. BUD COLLINS

I loved that man more than I have ever loved any
man, and we had a wonderful relationship. One day
I came home from school—at around the age of
eight—and I said, "Hey, Pop, I have to fill out these
cards and what am I, am I Catholic or Protestant or
what?" And he said, "Oh, I'll fill it out for you, son."
And then I asked, "What nationality am I, Pop, am
I Mexican, am I Irish, what am I?" He said, "Never
mind, I'll fill it out for you." So at school I gave it
to the teacher and she opened them all up and she
looked at me and she said, "Tony, did you fill this
out?" and I said, "I'm sorry, I didn't have all the
information so I asked my father to fill it out for
me." She said, "Your father says that you're Hindu,
Protestant, Catholic, Islamic, Jewish . . . he put down
all the religions of the world. How can you be that?
And here, you're Hungarian, you're Turkish, you're
Arab, you're French, you're Irish, you're Greek . . ."
And that became my life. I, out of nowhere, have
become that man because I have played the great
Arab leaders, I've become a Greek, I've played Chinese, I've been a priest, I've been the Pope—and
I feel perfectly comfortable in doing them. When
somebody says to me, "What religion are you?" I feel
like saying, "All of them." ANTHONY QUINN

I asked my father, "Pop, do you feel Mexican?" and
he said, "I feel Mexican, I feel Irish, I feel Russian,

I feel Arabic—I'm a man of the earth."
> LORENZO QUINN of his father, Anthony Quinn

I just came across a photograph of my eleventh
birthday party, which boasted a Hawaiian luau
theme. My younger sister and I wore real grass
skirts, plastic leis, and flowered bikini tops.

My father wore . . . well, practically nothing. He
wrapped the bottom half of his body in a wild flow-
ery fabric, donned a straight black wig, and carried
a spear. On his nose (looking like it went *through* his
nostrils) he sported a bone carved out of balsa wood.

The picture brought back that old surge of daddy
worship. "Dad," I thought tearfully, "you were such
a show-off!"

Other people, even those who loved him, had different names for my father's affliction—goofball,
asshole, blowhard, nut, idiot. "The first idiot jumping out of the airplane is your father," my mother
told me when I was eight and we were waiting on a
weedy field to see him parachute through the sky.

Being a show-off was a full time hobby for my
father, and I adored him for it. He wasn't a typical
life-of-the-party type, just a guy whose head was
filled with really high concepts all the time. One
Christmas he spent hours painstakingly gluing
lumps of coal to boxes so that he could present my
mother with five layers of empty coal-covered pack-
ages to open before she found a ring in the last
box. At Halloween he went out trick-or-treating as a
protestor against our town's failure to build a septic
system. "Your Relief Is Your Neighbor's Grief" said
one of his elaborate signs, and he carried a bedpan
for the candy.

As I get older I marvel at his high energy level.

Was it Nature's gift to someone destined to depart the planet early? He died at forty-seven and yet managed to start an electronics company, become an amateur radio operator (a ham), get a private pilot's and a glider license, build and operate a nineteenth-century blacksmith shop, press his own cider, maintain a collection of hit-and-miss engines, make his own wine, grow his own watermelon, and travel to Europe several times a year. Yet when my dog killed my parakeet, he somehow had the time to go into the company machine shop and make up a gleaming stainless steel tombstone engraved with SKIPPY 1961–1963.

His nuttiness meshed perfectly with his engineer's training and precision. One year Daddy bought a fifteen-foot Christmas tree and cut off the top. After positioning the bottom part of the tree in front of our big picture window inside, he scrambled up onto the roof with the top half and set it up directly in line with the inside section. Then he strung the lights in exactly the same way top and bottom, giving me a glorious few days of regaling the neighborhood kids with stories of how we had sawed a hole through the roof for our enormous tree.

One winter morning when I was nine, my dad watched me pull on my long green stocking cap and then he took me aside. "Here's an idea—I bet if you stuffed it with newspaper it would stand up straight." Five minutes later, I set off for school looking like some mutant elf, and of course all hell broke loose when I showed up on the playground appearing two feet taller than normal. Some really scary boys tried to knock my hat off, and I got called in and yelled at by the teacher, who said I was making a display of myself, which, as it turns out, has become a life-long hobby for me, too. CATHY CRIMMINS

Kurt Vonnegut

from

Fates Worse Than Death

When my father was sixty-five and I was twenty-seven, I said to him, thinking him a very old man, that it must have been fun for him to be an architect. He replied unexpectedly that it had been no fun at all, since architecture had everything to do with accounting and nothing to do with art. I felt that he had mousetrapped me, since he had encouraged me up until that moment to believe that architecture for him had indeed been a lark.

I now perceive his deception, so suddenly discontinued, as having been a high order of gallantry. While my two siblings and I were growing up, he gave us the illusion that our father was jauntily content with his professional past and excited about all the tough but amusing challenges still to come. The truth was that the Great Depression and then World War II, during which almost all building stopped, came close to gutting him as an architect. From the time he was forty-five until he was sixty-one he had almost no work. In prosperous times those would

186

have been his best years, when his evident gifts, reputation, and maturity might have caused some imaginative client to feel that Father was entitled to reach, even in Indianapolis, for greatness or, if you will, for soul-deep fun.

I am not about to speak of soup kitchens, much in the news again of late. We never missed a meal during the Great Depression. But Father had to close down his office, started up by *his* father, the first licensed architect in Indiana, and let his six employees go. Small jobs still came his way now and then, jobs so uninteresting, I now understand, that they would have been soporific to a high school drafting class. If we hadn't needed the money, Father might have said what I heard him say to a would-be client after World War II, when prosperity had returned to the land: "Why don't you get some pencils and squared paper, and see what you and your wife can do?" He said this pleasantly. He was trying to be helpful.

During the war he stopped being an architect entirely, and went to work in inventory control at the Atkins Saw Company, which was making weapons of some sort, maybe bayonets. It was then that his wife died. It became clear to him, too, that none of his three children would live in Indianapolis when the war was over. We would be following careers which would require us to live far away. So he was all but gutted yet again.

When prosperity, but not his children, returned to Indianapolis, Father became a partner of much younger men in a new architectural firm. His reputation was still excellent, and he was one of the most universally loved men in town, a founder, by the way, of the city's now world-famous Children's Museum. He was especially admired for his design of the Bell Telephone headquarters on North Meridian Street, a project conceived before the stock market crash.

After the war, Bell Telephone resolved to add more floors to the building, their exteriors to be identical with those of the eight below. They hired another architect, although Father was not senile or alcoholic or in any other way impaired. To Bell Telephone, an architect was an architect. Bell got the job done and it looked OK. So much for the romance of architecture.

Father retired alone to Brown County, Indiana, soon after that, to spend the rest of his life as a potter. He built his own potter's wheel. He died down there in the hills in 1957, at the age of seventy-two.

When I try to remember now what he was like when I was growing up and he had so little satisfying work to do, I see him as Sleeping Beauty, dormant in a brier patch, waiting for a prince. And it is easy to jump from that thought to this one: All architects I have known, in good times or bad, have seemed to be waiting forever for a generous, loving client who will let them become the elated artists they were born to be.

So my father's life might be seen as a particularly lugubrious fairy tale. He was Sleeping Beauty, and in 1929 not one but several princes, including Bell Telephone, had begun to hack through the briers to wake him up. But then they all got sick for sixteen years. And while they were in the hospital a wicked witch turned Sleeping Beauty into Rip Van Winkle instead.

When the Depression hit I was taken out of private school and put into public school. So I had a new set of friends to bring home to have a look at

whatever my father was. These were the ten-year-
old children of the yeomanry of Hoosierdom, and it
was they who first told me that my father was as
exotic as a unicorn.

In an era when men of his class wore dark suits and
white shirts and monochromatic neckties, Father appeared to have outfitted himself at the Salvation
Army. Nothing matched. I understand now, of
course, that he had selected the elements of his costume with care, that the colors and textures were
juxtaposed so as to be interesting and, finally,
beautiful.

While other fathers were speaking gloomily of
coal and iron and grain and lumber and cement and
so on, and yes, of Hitler and Mussolini, too, my father was urging friends and startled strangers alike
to pay attention to some object close at hand,
whether natural or manmade, and to celebrate it as
a masterpiece. When I took up the clarinet, he de-
clared the instrument, black studded with silver, to
be a masterpiece. Never mind whether it could make
music or not. He adored chess sets, although he
could not play that game worth a nickel. My new
friends and I brought him a moth one time, wanting
to know what sort of moth it was. He said that he
did not know its name, but that we could all agree
wholeheartedly on this much: that it was a masterpiece.

And he was the first planetary citizen my new
friends had ever seen, and possibly the last one, too.
He was no more a respecter of politics and national
boundaries than (that image again) a unicorn. Beauty
could be found or created anywhere on this planet,
and that was that.

AT&T has completed yet another building, this
one on the island of Manhattan, near where I live.
The telephone company has again done without the

services of my father, who could not now be awakened in any case. AT&T hired Philip Johnson instead, a Sleeping Beauty who throughout his adult
life has been tickled awake by ardent princes.

Should I now rage at Fate for not having enabled
my father to have as much fun as Mr. Johnson?

I try to imagine my father speaking to me across
the abyss between the dead and the living, and I
hear him saying this: "Do not pity me because I in
my prime awaited romantic challenges which never
came. If you wish to carve an epitaph on my modest
headstone in Crown Hill Cemetery at this late date,
then let it be this: IT WAS ENOUGH TO HAVE BEEN A
UNICORN."

Stanley Elkin

My Father's Life

All children's parents are too complicated for them. Certainly my father was too complicated for me. Love, like an obstacle, gets in the way. We know them too early. Then they die.

What he left me—I was going on twenty-eight, he on fifty-five—wasn't money so much as a pride in money, its powers of ratification, its green nod, all its Checkpoint Charlie majestics and corroboratives, all its gracious, sweet safe-conducts. The rich were all right in his book, as they are in mine, as, finally, *he* is in mine. (What he left in me broken, distorted, lapsed, the wear and tear of capital. To this day I am too much in awe of them, the really moneyed, not jealous but deferential, my tied tongue like the submission signal of some forest animal.)

My father earned around $50,000 a year in the 1940s. (There's nothing to astrology, its cusps and houses, its star swirl like thumbprint or snowstorm, astral influence like the pull of a tide, but people have their prime times, I think, their cycles, their

191

seven-fat, seven-lean-years menses and runs of luck. The forties were my father's decade. He looked like a man of the forties. The shaped fedora and the fresh haircut and the shined shoes. He was handsome, I mean. Like an actor in a diplomat's part, a star-crossed Secretary of State, say. Phil *looked* romantic. The noblesse oblige of his smile and the faint melodrama of the poses he struck in mirrors. His soft silver hair, gray since his 20s, the dark, carefully trimmed mustache, the widow's peak, the long patrician features, his good cheekbones like drawn swords. The vague rakishness of his face like a kind of wink. He was a traveling salesman, a rhinestone merchant, purveyor of costume jewelry to the trade. He worked in the Chicago offices of the old Great Northern Building at State and Jackson for Coro, Inc., which, in its time, was the largest manufacturer of "junk" jewelry in the world, and his territory was, well, immense, most of the Midwest—Wisconsin, Iowa, Minnesota, the Dakotas, Michigan but not Detroit, Illinois but not Chicago, Indiana but not Indianapolis, Missouri but not Kansas City or St. Louis. Some odd lot, under three flags arrangement of compromised spoils he had with Coro's New York headquarters like the divvy of armies of occupation. It was big enough, at any rate, to keep him on the road two months out of three—though he often managed to get home weekends—and when one heart attack too many forced him to slow down in the fifties, he had to hire three men to cover the ground for him while he stayed in the Great Northern in Chicago and worked the phones.

Calling the buyers, calling them darling, calling them sweetheart, calling them dear. And how much was *shmooz* and how much traveling salesman's protocol and how much true romance I really can't say.

Though some was. Some must have been, I think. He must have been irresistible to those Minnesota and Indiana ladies. Wisconsin farmers' daughters, the girls of the Dakotas, the Michigan peninsular. Though maybe not. He didn't frequent bars; would have looked, and felt, out of place in the rough taverns where farmers and fishermen and hunters traded the time of day and did the shoptalk of field and stream, the gauge of a shotgun shell the test of a line. Would have hesitated to ask for rye, his drink and bread of choice. So not only can I not really say, I don't really know. He was no Willy Loman. I never asked him, "What happened in Philly, Philly?"

Nor would those farmers have understood *his* shoptalk—the spring and fall seasons something different to them than they were to him. Nor understood his enthusiasm for costume jewelry, interesting to him as treasure chest, pieces of eight—the paste pearl and glass gem, all the colored chips and beads of his trade, amorphous as platelets seen under a microscope, all the crystalline shards of the blood's streaming what the kaleidoscope saw, the bright complicated jigsaw of the toy realities, random and patchwork as a quilt.

Proud of how much money he earned, proud of his wit, his Hester Street smarts.

The price of admission to the movies when my father was a kid was three cents, two for a nickel. He would range up and down the line calling, "I've got two cents; who's got three? I've got two; who's got three?"

Here are more traveling salesman stories.

When he first went on the road for Coro at the beginning of the Depression, my father worked out of New York City on a $35-a-week draw against commission, was given the clapboard and red-brick small towns of upstate New York for his territory. One day Mr. Rosenberger, the firm's president, called him into his office and told him that he was into the company for $200 or $300.

"I know," said my father.

"You know?"

"Sure," my father said. "This time next month it'll be another fifty dollars. In two months maybe another hundred more. In three more months it could be double what I owe you now. If I don't quit or you don't fire me, sooner or later I could bankrupt this company."

"Maybe I'd better fire you, then."

"Sure," my father said, "or give me a territory that isn't played out. Where the stores aren't all boarded up and the town's leading industry ain't torn shoelaces or selling apples by the bite."

It's the language of myth and risk and men sizing each other up. It's steely-eyed appraisal talk, I-like-the-cut-of-your-jib speech, and maybe that's not the way it happened. But that was the way my father told it and it became The Story of How They Gave Him the Central Standard Time Zone—"I've got two; who's got three? I've got two; who's got three?"—of how he moved west and took up his manifest destiny in the Chicago office.

This was the thirties and the beginning of my father's itinerancy on the road—it's the American metaphor—to his luck. (Automobiles he used, berths, compartments on trains, and once, during the war, he rode back to Chicago from Minneapolis in a caboose, and was possibly one of the first salesmen to use airplanes regularly. There were, I recall, preferred-customer cards from airlines in his wallets—and recall the wallets, too, their fat leather smoothed to use, all his leathers, his luggage and dop kits.) Some golden age of the personal we shared through his stories, his actor's resonances, all those anecdotes of self-dramatizing exigency, of strut and shuffle and leap and roll. In those days it was his America. . . .

We closed our apartment in the summers and went east, and one time—this would have been the forties, the last year of the war—I was staying over in Manhattan with my dad. (Though we had a place in Jersey, my father came out only on weekends and spent the rest of the week in one of the hotels around Herald Square near Coro's New York office—the Pennsylvania, the McAlpin, the Vanderbilt.) And this particular morning he was running late and said we would grab a quick breakfast at the Automat.

I was following him in the cafeteria line and the girl behind the counter asked what he wanted.

"Scrambled eggs," he said. "And some bacon."

"Bacon is extra," she said.

I thought he was going to hit her. He slammed his tray down and started to yell, to call her names.

"Goddamn you!" he shouted. "You stupid ass! Did I *ask* if bacon was extra? Do I *look* as if I can't afford extra goddamn bacon? *Who in the hell do you think you are?*"

"Take it easy, mister," said someone behind us in line. "What do you want from her? She didn't mean anything."

"You shut up," my father warned him, "you shut up and mind your goddamn business!"

And the fellow did, terrified of the crazy man ahead of him in line. Then my father shoved some bills onto the counter and pulled me away.

I want to be careful here. What he did was terrible. He was something of a snob who didn't much

care for what he would never have called "the element," but who may have thought like that, who
had by heart in his head some personalized complex
periodic table of the four-flusher fraudulent. (The
element, yes, who traded in pseudo elements, in
fractions and grosses of the manque, the plated silver and the short karat.) But that woman had hit
him where he lived, had touched some still-raw, up-
from-Hester Street vulnerability he must have fa-
vored like a game leg. It was awful to see, but today
I am sorrier for my father than I am for the woman.
He *hated* four-flushers—it was the worst thing he
could call you—and the thought that that woman
behind the counter suspected something like that in
him drove him, I think, temporarily insane. If they'd
understood, no jury in the world would even have
been *permitted* to convict him.

The other side of the coin is braver, his intact I've-
got-two-who's-got-three instincts.

It was probably one of his milder heart attacks.
He was to be discharged from the hospital that
morning and my mother drove down from the
North Side to fetch him home.

"How are you feeling?" his doctor asked.

"Not bad. A little shaky. Pretty good."

"You'll have to take it easy for a few weeks."

"Sure."

"Even after you go back to work I don't think you
should drive for a while."

"Hey," my father said, "I know the drill."

When my mother brought the car around from
the hospital lot he asked for the keys.

"Phil," said my mother, "you heard what he said."

"Come on, Tootsie. Give me the keys."

"But you're not supp—"

"Tootsie," he said, "give me the damn car keys."

The drive on the Outer Drive from the South to the North Side was practically a straight shot. There was this one stoplight, on Oak Street, in the few-hundred-north block. My father was a good driver but he looked at you when he spoke and was as much the raconteur in a moving automobile as in a living room. He could turn anything into an anecdote and he delighted in the voices, in the gestures. He was telling my mother a story and waving his arm about.

"Phil," she screamed, "the light!"

"What? Oh," he said, "yeah."

He continued to tell his story while waiting for the long light to change on Oak Street. Oldsmobiles in neutral have a tendency to creep. The impact wasn't great but it infuriated the other driver. He came pouring out of his car like a dirge, like a requiem mass, a big, beefy six-footer. He pulled the car door open on the driver's side and started to curse my father, who simply reached his hand into the inside pocket of his suit coat and held it there around an imaginary gun. He interrupted the big man's angry obscenities.

"Get back in your car," my father told him quietly. "I'm counting to five. I'm not even bothering to count out loud."

The man held his arms up and backed off. Back in his car he ran the light. When it turned green again my father drove home.

When I was either seven or eight I bought my father a plaster-of-paris reproduction of the Statue of Liberty. It was more than a foot high and the torch was really a cigarette lighter. He took it out of the paper cone in which it had been wrapped like a rose and wanted to know where the hell I'd gotten such crap.

People, tender of the kiddy sensibilities, are appalled by his callousness and profess not to believe me when I tell them that I was grateful, at least after thinking it over. It was educational, a lesson in taste. I buy neither souvenirs nor novelty items. No pillows with ATLANTIC CITY embroidered in satin have ever graced my sofas. No miniature outhouses are as frontlets between my eyes, nor is there anything like them on the lintels of my house or on my gates. . . .

. . . Often, when my father went to New York, he would visit his sister Jean. One night when my cousin Bert came back from law school my father was in my aunt's apartment. She'd given him some supper and he'd gone to the sofa to lie down. He was moaning and Jean asked if he was uncomfortable, if there was anything she could do. (It was the 1950s now, the decade of his heart attacks, four in seven years, and he would wake up coughing in the middle of the night, hawking, hacking, trying with those terrible percussives to bring up the poisons from his flooded chest; it was the fifties now, the decade of his pain and death.) "You work too hard, Phil. You'll kill yourself, working so hard. Slow down; take it easy. So you make a little less money. Your health is what matters."

My father said something she couldn't understand, and she leaned down to understand him better. "What, Phil? What's that?"

"My health," he said scornfully, louder now, and Bert could hear him, too. "Listen," he said, "if I have to live on ten thousand a year like some ribbon clerk I don't *want* to live."

So, maybe, in the long run, it ain't more blessed to give than receive; maybe picking up checks all 'round is not only hazardous to your health but disastrous to your character. But maybe he knew that and picked up the checks anyway, who behind his glass-jaw sensibilities only wanted another shot at that line, to be on it again, the roles reversed this time, what he really wanted only to call, "*I've* got three! *I've* got three; who's got two?"

QUALITY TIME

My dad and I would spend Sunday mornings in the breakfast room. Me and my dad: it was our time together and usually it was just the two of us. And occasionally Charlie.

There we'd be, in the gentle morning light, with the sun slipping through the colored circles in the bottle-glass windows, tossing brilliant spots of blues and greens across the gleaming oakwood floor. From the kitchen floated whiffs of waffles, smells of sausage and, on Sundays, Swedish pancakes heaped with lingonberries twinkling like rubies. My father was a life-long Swedish loyalist, and the Swedish pancakes arrived in the hands of Simon, the Swedish house-man, hot off the griddle of Aina, the Swedish cook.

Life was good for me and my dad in that breakfast room: big, blond people moving softly, reassuringly through a string of golden mornings. And there we were, in our secret Scandinavia, just like a perfect couple, you know, unless Charlie or someone was there.

When Charlie was there, my dad would sit him on one knee and me on the other and he'd put his hand on both our necks, and when he squeezed my neck, I'd move my mouth, and when he squeezed Charlie's neck, he'd move his. As Charlie and I yammered away at each other across my father, mouths flapping soundlessly, behind us, smiling politely, sat my dad, happily speaking for both of us.

CANDICE BERGEN

I was raised in the Baptist church, and every Sunday I'd sit in the kitchen with my dad, trying to get him to go to church. My dad smokin' some old Luckys, you know, drinkin' a beer. Sayin', "Aw, babe, don't worry about the old man." LILY TOMLIN

We had a great time together. I'm an only child, and he started tutoring me when I was a little kid. I'd sit on his lap and I'd drive him nuts with the Sunday paper. I'd make him do voices for all his characters, and then I'd say, "Can you do Prince Valiant or Dick Tracy or the Katzenjammer Kids?" I'd drive him crazy. NOEL BLANC of his father, Mel Blanc

My father was an M.D. and a surgeon, and he used to take me on house calls. I grew up in a farm community, and many of these trips were way out in the country, so we had lots of time in the car. That's where we really talked to each other.

BOB MATHIAS

He and I started riding motorcycles at the same time. I was fifteen, he was fifty.
TIMOTHY FORBES of his father, Malcolm S. Forbes

Dad let me know that he was aware of being too often an absentee father, and he looked for every chance to take me fishing or hunting on Saturdays. These were cherished times for privacy, exchanges of confidences, and learning outdoor skills from my father, the teacher. He could read sky and wind, and he was good at anticipating weather changes. He knew the significance of cloudy water, sensing where fish would hide. He lectured on their movements and habitats and on the differences between redfish, catfish, sunfish, and speckled trout. He walked with his head up to gauge wind and perhaps to stop cold for a deer or a covey of quail.

Father had what I later, in Vietnam, came to know as "jungle eye"—the ability to see tiny movements, frame by frame, even to follow insects.

The quiet hours of such a day, a world away from people and pressures, produced indescribable euphoria in us both. I had this liberating sense of running free. I was conscious of Father's chest expanding, the triangle around his eyes opening up to relax, the sense of camaraderie between us. Spotting a run of speckled trout, he'd light up and display a look of sheer joy. DAN RATHER

My father took me fishing once. He marched me to the riverbank and snapped a picture of me with a fishing rod in my hand, then we went home.
ANDREI CODRESCU

When I was around seven or eight, we went fishing and couldn't catch anything, so Dad took out his machine gun and said, "You know what? We'll shoot 'em." He let me pull the trigger. "Well, we still didn't get any," Dad said afterward. "But we scared the hell out of 'em."

> JACK FLOYD of his father,
> Charles Arthur "Pretty Boy" Floyd

I assumed that my father was away from the store having lunch, as he always did in the middle of Saturday afternoons; I was therefore suddenly shaken by the sight of him opening the back door, then walking toward me with a frown on his face. Not knowing what to do, but nonetheless compelled by nervous energy to do *something*, I quickly took the ball in my right hand, cocked my arm, and threw it at him.

The ball soared forty feet in a high arc toward his head. He was so startled to see it coming that he halted his step and stared skittishly up at the sky through his steel-rimmed glasses. Then—as if not knowing whether to block the ball or try to catch it—he extended his arms upward and cupped his soft tailors' hands, and braced himself for the impact.

I stood watching anxiously from the far corner of the lot, no less shocked than he that I had chosen this moment to confront him—perhaps for the first time in his life—with the challenge of catching a ball. I cringed as I saw the ball hit him solidly on the side of the neck, carom off a shoulder, rebound against the wall behind him, and come rolling slowly back to his feet, where it finally stopped.

As I waited, holding my breath, he lowered his

head and began to rub his neck. Then, seeing the ball at his feet he stooped to pick it up. For a moment he held the rubber ball in his right hand and examined it as if it were a strange object. He squeezed it. He turned it around in his fingers. Finally, with a bashful smile, he turned toward me, cocked his arm awkwardly, and tried to throw the ball in my direction. GAY TALESE

I can remember playing under the big wooden desk in his office. My mother didn't like us to chew gum, so we'd go into his office and he'd feed us gum under the desk. JOHN F. KENNEDY, JR.

The first time I got totally shit-faced, I was drinking beer in a Bohemian social club with my daddy at the age of nine. Dad drove me back to my grandmother's house and made me sleep it off in the car before I could go inside. Mama Nelson would have kicked the shit out of both of us. WILLIE NELSON

I was introduced to religion on Saturday night. I don't recall just when, but as far back as I can remember, Saturday night was the Lord's night in our house. Whenever Dad was able to make it home on his own two feet, he would bring a recording of a spiritual, a plate of pigs' feet and potato salad from the corner delicatessen or a plate of fish-and-chips from the wine joint around the corner, and whatever was left of his last bottle of religion. He usually got home about three o'clock in the morning, and the moment he hit the block I could hear him singing (or yelling) the record he had. By the time he got upstairs, everybody in the building knew the song and hated it. Before Dad was in the house, I could hear him calling me.

By the time he finished unlocking and relocking the door at least six times, kicking on it, cursing out the lock and the neighbors who had tried to quiet him down, I was up and had already turned on the phonograph. On her way to the door, Mama would say, "Boy, turn that thing off and git back in bed." While Mama told Dad how disgusting he was, I would be busily picking out the pig's feet and fish-and-chips with the least amount of hot sauce on them. When Mama had gotten tired of competing with Dad's singing, she went back to bed. As Dad gave me the record—usually by Sister Rosetta Tharpe, the Dixie Hummingbirds, or the Four Blind Boys— he would tell me how somebody I had never heard of sang it in the cotton fields or at somebody's wedding or funeral "down home." After listening to the record at least a dozen times, Dad would turn the phonograph off, and we would sing the song a few times. Before dawn started sneaking through the windows, Dad and I had gone through his entire repertoire of spirituals. By daybreak, we were both drunk and had fallen on the floor, and we stayed there until we awoke later in the day.

CLAUDE BROWN

My father and I were watching the Giants play the Colts in the snow for the championship when two Connecticut state troopers arrived during the first sudden death overtime. They watched with us till the game ended, then took my father to the lockup in Danbury. He had left a bad check at The Three Bears; they were pressing charges.

GEOFFREY WOLFF

When we lived in San Francisco—this would have been in the late 1950s—my father would get off work very late at night and he would come home and nap more than sleep because he was still keyed up, and then early in the morning he would take me to a movie theater that showed nothing but cartoons. I would sit there gaga over these cartoons and my father would be snoring away. A few doors down the block from the movie theater there was a store that sold marzipan candy—made in all shapes and sizes, like little Swiss chalets, for example. But my favorites, *our* favorites, were the ones in the shape of dog turds and vomitus. They actually had marzipan candy that looked like dog turds and vomitus! So, of course, it gave us great pleasure to go in and buy a couple of marzipan dog turds and walk out eating them like they were ice cream cones while people stared at us on the street.

Another time we bought the marzipan vomitus and we came back to our apartment and my father sent me running into the living room saying, "Mommy, Mommy, Daddy's sick." She ran into the kitchen to see my father with a pained expression on his face, doubled over, and the marzipan vomitus. My mother said, "Oh, Ernie, now don't worry, I'll take care of this." And then my father reached over and said, "Oh, that's okay, Patty, honey," picked up the marzipan vomitus and took a bite out of it. To this day I can hear my mother going, "Aaaaagh."

I've wondered, over the years, as I've recalled these moments with my father, what they're supposed to teach me about life. I can't say there's any lesson, except the sheer pleasure of his company, which was a great gift, and which I gather is sometimes hard to come by between fathers and sons.

SCOTT SIMON

After he had read me the first chapter of *Swiss Family Robinson* one Sunday night he sent me to bed, and stayed up until dawn finishing the book. The next time he was going to read aloud to me I brought out *Swiss Family Robinson* again. But Groucho returned it to the shelf and selected *Jack the Giant Killer*.

When I asked why, he said, "I've already finished *Swiss Family Robinson*. I'll tell you how it comes out. You wouldn't like the middle part, anyway. It's too good for children."

So he gave me a quick synopsis of it, and we were on to *Jack the Giant Killer*. He didn't have time to waste reading the same book twice.

ARTHUR MARX of his father, Groucho Marx

My dad and I once went down to Taxco, Mexico, for the purpose of reading aloud to each other G. K. Chesterton's *Orthodoxy*.

CHRISTOPHER BUCKLEY of his father, William F. Buckley, Jr.

I remember him getting up at five-thirty in the morning, pipe already in mouth, tweed jacket on shoulders, and driving me in full hockey regalia to the ice rink to play Pee-Wee hockey. He would sit in the cold for the next two hours, reading Johnson, while I would be battering people with my skates and my sticks, trying to get into a fight. We would both arrive back at the house a few hours later quite happy.   SAM FUSSELL of his father, Paul Fussell

At the end of long summer holidays at the age of sixteen or seventeen, I was going back to Eton, and the last night we sat up late talking in the study at Chartwell. We talked of many things until one or one-thirty in the morning, and then he said, "You know, dear boy, I think I've talked to you more these holidays than my father talked to me in the whole of his life." There was no bitterness in it, but there was sadness.

RANDOLPH CHURCHILL of his father,
Winston Churchill

G. Gordon Liddy

from

Will

My father and I did the things other fathers and
sons did too. He took me to the big league baseball
games and taught me that the best players are the
smartest players. It is permissible, my father taught,
to make an occasional physical error. It is never permissible to make a mental error, in baseball or anything else. To my father, the intellect was and must
be supreme. From my earliest memory to the last
day I saw him alive, if I made an error in his presence in English usage (or Latin or German, for that
matter), he would correct me on the spot.

Years after I became an adult, my father told me
that not once in his life had *his* father ever hugged
him or shown him any similar sign of affection. Yet
I knew my father had loved his father dearly, acting
as his night nurse for more than a year as he died
of cancer. As a consequence, my father tried to hug
me often, but it always seemed to me that that was
just what he was doing; *trying* to hug me, wanting to
but not knowing how, as if never having been the

object of a fatherly embrace himself, he could not pass on what he had never received.

In fairness to my father, I stress that this is a subjective impression. The fact of the matter is that he *did* hug me, often, and it may well have been that my self-loathing, born of contempt for my weakness in the face of fear, rendered me unable to recognize genuine fatherly affection and to receive it when offered.

My father had a strong personality, yet he had a genius for being assertive without offending others. Early in my life he let me know that he was not interested in any tales I might carry to him about others and had no use for "snitching." He hated lying and taught that it made impossible the mutual confidence necessary for any enterprise among men. "If you don't want somebody to know something," he said, "just don't speak to them about it. Never lie." As for tale carrying, he was blunt. "I am very interested in whatever you have to say for yourself. Others can speak for themselves." A man known for his loyalty to his benefactors, he taught me that a man does "not extricate himself from difficulty at the expense of his associates."

As I grew older and the winning of countless battles with myself produced an increasingly strong personality, my father and I would clash. Yet we loved each other greatly and I have never respected any man more than I did my father. Nevertheless our relationship was, from its inception, almost formal. An example would be the matter of baseball.

Baseball was my father's favorite sport. I enjoyed it well enough, but it was not *my* favorite sport. My father, who excelled at baseball as he did in almost everything he tried, wanted me to excel at it too. It was good for the body and good for the mind. By the time I was eight years old, I resisted playing baseball with him. I'd play stoopball and stickball with other boys on the block and play it well, but I was reluctant to play baseball with or under the direction of my father. I just couldn't play it well enough; that is to say, perfectly.

In the spring of 1940, when I was nine, my father stressed how much he was looking forward to the coming baseball season. Again I expressed my reluctance but my father, the persuasive advocate, talked me into another season of the sport. It was symbolic of our relationship that this agreement took the form of a written contract which both my mother and seven-year-old sister solemnly signed as witnesses. I still have that contract:

CONTRACT

THIS AGREEMENT made this 15th day of March, 1940, by and between GEORGE GORDON BATTLE LIDDY, party of the first part, hereinafter termed "Player," and SYLVESTER J. LIDDY, party of the second part, hereinafter termed "Manager";

WITNESSETH

NOW, THEREFORE, THIS INDENTURE WITNESSETH that for and in consideration of the sum of One Dollar ($1.00) and other good and valuable consideration, paid by the party of the first part, Player, to the party of the second part, Manager, the receipt of which is hereby acknowledged, the parties hereto agree as follows:

1. The Player agrees to play baseball for the coming season of 1940 exclusively for and under the management of the party of the second part as Manager.

2. The party of the second part, Manager, agrees to furnish to the party of the first part, Player, all necessary baseball equipment which may be required for the coming season.

3. The party of the first part, Player, agrees to follow instructions, advice and orders of the party of the second part, Manager, at all times except when the Player is at bat during a regular game and he has a count of three balls and two strikes, he may then use his own best judgment.

4. During the baseball season and during spring training season, the party of the first part, Player, agrees to go to bed every night not later than 8:30 P.M. promptly.

5. The party of the first part, Player, further agrees to eat all his meals regularly and promptly and such foods as Manager may select for him, or if he should be at Camp during part of the baseball season, such foods as the Camp Directors may order.

6. Spring training, weather permitting, is to begin on March 21st, 1940.

IN WITNESS WHEREOF we hereunto sign our names and affix our seals at Hoboken, in the County of Hudson and State of New Jersey, this 15th day of March, 1940.

WITNESS:

Maria C. Liddy   *George Gordon Battle Liddy*

WITNESS:

Margaret Liddy   *Sylvester J. Liddy [L.S.]*

A deal is a deal and on 21 March 1940 I reported to my father for spring training.

GOLDEN
MOMENTS

One of my most deeply imprinted memories of child-hood is being taken up in a small plane by my father: tightly buckled in the front seat of a two-seater Piper Cub as my father in the cockpit behind me taxis us along the bumpy runway of a small country airport outside Lockport [New York] . . . and suddenly the rattling plane leaves the ground, lifts above a line of trees at the end of the runway . . . climbing, banking, miraculously riding the air currents . . . until the roar-ing noise of the engine seems to subside, and we're airborne, and below is a familiar landscape made in-creasingly exotic as we climb. Transit Road and its traffic . . . farmland, wooded land, hedgerows . . . houses, barns, pastureland, intersecting roads . . . creeks and streams . . . and the sky opening above us oceanic, unfathomable. JOYCE CAROL OATES

I first water-skied next to my dad in 1954, near Dal-las. It was the happiest day of my short life.
ROCK BRYNNER of his father, Yul Brynner

I remember the first time I heard my own voice. It was the early fifties and all they had were wire recorders. I would do some recording and I remember my dad's sentence, "Now let's play it back."

ART GARFUNKEL

I guess my favorite memories are of having a father. I have a whole five years of memories. I remember when Alice the cat died and my father was crying; I remember watching TV with him; wrestling and jumping up and down with him in my room; going to Central Park and riding in the horse carriage together. We did a lot of drawing. He would scribble in circles and squiggles on a piece of paper, and I would have to turn it into whatever I saw in them. We took turns doing it to see who could make more things out of the squiggles. That was a game I loved to play. With him, every day was an adventure. It was like my dad and I were buddies, and there was no real sorrow then.

SEAN LENNON

His name was Ernie Simon. He was a comedian and he was also the field announcer for the Cleveland Indians, which was just something he fell into and did part time for his love of sports. He was primarily a comedian. He died in 1968, when he was forty-eight and I was sixteen. Some years ago I was moving from one apartment to another and I found some old audio tapes that had been made on one of the earliest tape recorders, a Revere, I think. My father had gotten the machine to practice his routines, but of course he began to use it for family matters, and the tapes are more valuable than old family pictures.

There's a scene where, one Christmas, I was two years old and we were around the Christmas tree and you hear some kind of music box playing in the background and you hear my mother showing me the little scene underneath the tree and she says, "Here's the bull and the steer and the camel, here are the wise men and here are Joseph and Mary, and do we know who this is?" And I say, "Baby Jesus!" My father was Jewish and my mother Catholic, one of those hybrid combinations. And she said, "Christmas is Baby Jesus's birthday, why don't we sing happy birthday to Baby Jesus?" So you hear my mother singing: "Happy birthday to you, happy birthday to you, happy birthday, Baby Jesus, happy birthday to you." Then you hear my father's voice come in: "For he's a jolly good fellow, for he's a jolly good fellow. . . ." The memory of that gives me a great deal of pleasure. SCOTT SIMON

My father had always been a heavy gambler, but he always won, so it wasn't so bad as it might have been. He was an expert poker player, and he won even when very drunk. Sometimes when most drunk he won fantastic things. He won a Stanley Steamer gambling, and once he won a boudoir set in ebony and silver with every conceivable kind of brush and hoe and lance and stabber for fingernails and toenails, both male and female, and all sorts of pomade pots and perfume bottles of cut-crystal with silver and ebony inlay and multiple mirrors of curious construction. All laid out, it filled the boudoir and all the table tops and shelves in my father's dressing room as well. He came home hilariously drunk in a taxi with a trunkful of this stuff at four o'clock one morning. He routed us out of bed and spread it all over the hall floor. At first my mother was a little miffed at being awakened; then she was amused, and as more and more implements kept appearing she was overwhelmed. She took a couple of drinks herself and at last we all romped around brushing and manicuring each other in the lavish hallway under the absurd chandeliers that blazed away on us as the dawn came in at the doors.

KENNETH REXROTH

I remember Riverview. This vast amusement park was located on Chicago's North Side. It was magnificent, dangerous, and thrilling. There were freak shows, there was the renowned Bob's roller coaster, the fastest in the world; there was the ROTOR, a room-sized cylinder in which one stood back against the wall and was spun around, while the floor dropped away; there was the PARACHUTE JUMP, the symbol of Riverview, and visible for a mile.

There was illicit gambling, one could die on the rides, the place reeked of sex. A trip to Riverview was more than a thrill, it was a dangerous dream adventure for the children and for their parents.

My father took me up in the Parachute Jump. We were slowly hoisted ten stories in the air, seated on a rickety board, and held in place by a frayed rope. We reached the top of the scaffold, the parachute dropped, the seat dropped out from under us, and my father said under his breath: "Jesus Christ, we're both going to die here."

I remember wondering why I was not terrified by his fear. I think I was proud to be sharing such a grown-up experience with him.   DAVID MAMET

The old man had hit on the daily double, and to celebrate we were going to opening day at Wrigley Field and sit in the grandstand. There were four of us in the group—the old man, Dutch Louis, Shaky Tony, and me.

It was a cold, blustery day, so everyone dressed accordingly—long underwear, wool pants, heavy jackets, and a pint of Jim Beam. Except me. I didn't get to wear Jim Beam because it was 1939 and I was six. The old man wasn't permissive.   MIKE ROYKO

One day after church, my dad and I were crossing Wilshire at Rodeo on our way to the M.F.K.S. coffee shop for prune danish, when we bumped into Gary Cooper.

Cooper spoke first. "How are you, Jack?" he drawled.

"I'm good, Coop," my dad said. "How're you?"

"I'm good, too," Coop replied.

They nodded at each other and we went on our way.   HOLLY PALANCE

(This page constitutes an extension of the copyright page.)

Permissions/Acknowledgments

From *Loyalties: A Son's Memoir* by Carl Bernstein, copyright ©
1989 by Carl Bernstein. Reprinted by permission of Simon &
Schuster.

From *Yul: The Man Who Would Be King* by Rock Brynner, copyright © 1989 by Rock Brynner. Reprinted by permission of
Simon & Schuster.

From *The Way I See It* by Patti Davis, copyright © 1992 by Patti
Davis. Reprinted by permission of the Putnam Publishing
Group.

From *Pieces of Soap* by Stanley Elkin, copyright © 1992 by Stanley Elkin. Reprinted by permission of Simon & Schuster, Inc.

From *The Remains of the Day* by Kazuo Ishiguro, copyright ©
1989 by Kazuo Ishiguro. Reprinted by permission of Alfred A.
Knopf, Inc.

From *Surprised by Joy* by C. S. Lewis, copyright © 1955 by C. S.
Lewis. Reprinted by permission of Harcourt Brace Jovanovich.

From *Will* by G. Gordon Liddy, copyright © 1980 by G. Gordon
Liddy. Reprinted by permission of St. Martin's Press.

From *Life With Groucho* by Arthur Marx, copyright © 1954 by
Arthur Marx. Reprinted by permission of the author and the
author's agents, Scott Meredith Literary Agency, Inc., 845 Third
Avenue, New York, New York 10022.

"Faerieland" by Colin McEnroe, copyright © 1992 by Colin
McEnroe. Originally in the *Hartford Courant*. Reprinted by permission of the author.

From *Rain Or Shine: A Family Memoir* by Cyra McFadden, copyright © 1986 by Cyra McFadden. Reprinted by permission of
Alfred A. Knopf, Inc.

From *Every Good-Bye Ain't Gone* by Itabari Njeri, copyright ©
1982, 1983, 1984, 1986, 1990 by Itabari Njeri. Reprinted by
permission of Times Books, a division of Random House, Inc.

"Fathers" from *Essays in Disguise* by Wilfrid Sheed, copyright ©

1990 by Wilfrid Sheed. Reprinted by permission of Alfred A. Knopf, Inc.

From *The Lost Father* by Mona Simpson, copyright © 1992 by Mona Simpson. Reprinted by permission of Alfred A. Knopf, Inc.

From *Unto the Sons* by Gay Talese, copyright © 1992 by Gay Talese. Reprinted by permission of Alfred A. Knopf, Inc.

From *Fates Worse Than Death* by Kurt Vonnegut, copyright © 1991 by Kurt Vonnegut. Reprinted by permission of the author.

From *John Wayne, My Father* by Aissa Wayne and Steve Delsohn, copyright © 1991 by Aissa Wayne and Steve Delsohn. Reprinted by permission of Random House, Inc.

"Grass" from *The Quest for Identity* by Allen Wheelis, copyright © 1958 by W.W. Norton & Company, Inc. Renewed 1986 by Allen Wheelis. Reprinted by permission of the author and W.W. Norton & Company, Inc.

From *Black Boy* by Richard Wright, copyright © 1937, 1942, 1944, 1945 by Richard Wright. Reprinted by permission of HarperCollins Publishers.

INDEX

221

PLUME 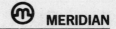 **MERIDIAN**

WORDS TO THE WISE

☐ **NO CHAIRS MAKE FOR SHORT MEETINGS** *And Other Business Maxims from Dad.* **by Richard Rybolt.** Over 150 of the author's timeless ideas and adages teach an effective business philosophy that every working person, from laborer to company president, can instantly understand and implement. From specific advice on beating out the competition to keeping one's priorities straight, this charming book is proof that nice guys can finish first.
(938737—$12.95)

☐ **FATHERS Compiled and Edited by Jon Winokur.** Bitter or sweet, sentimental and barbed—this compendium of anecdotes, quips, and essays celebrates famous names and ordinary folks. Candice Bergen, Arthur Ashe, Alice Walker, Thurgood Marshall, and more than 200 others remember their fathers to offer moving and humorous testimony to the enduring legacy of fathers.
(272076—$9.95)

☐ **THE WIT AND WISDOM OF WILL ROGERS Edited by Alex Ayres.** An entertaining book from a national resource whose wit and wisdom are as vital and valid today as when he delivered them. Filled with such memorable quotes as (on stocks): "Don't gamble; take all your savings and buy some good stock, then hold it till it goes up, then sell it. If it don't go up, don't buy it."
(011159—$10.00)

Prices slightly higher in Canada.

Buy them at your local bookstore or use this convenient coupon for ordering.

PENGUIN USA
P.O. Box 999, Dept. #17109
Bergenfield, New Jersey 07621

Please send me the books I have checked above.
I am enclosing $_____ (please add $2.00 to cover postage and handling).
Send check or money order (no cash or C.O.D.'s) or charge by Mastercard or VISA (with a $15.00 minimum). Prices and numbers are subject to change without notice.

Card # _____ Exp. Date _____
Signature _____
Name _____
Address _____
City _____ State _____ Zip Code _____

For faster service when ordering by credit card call **1-800-253-6476**

Allow a minimum of 4-6 weeks for delivery. This offer is subject to change without notice

THE OUTRAGEOUS WIT AND WISDOM OF JON WINOKUR

☐ **THE PORTABLE CURMUDGEON Compiled and Edited by Jon Winokur.** More than 1000 outrageously irreverent quotations, anecdotes, and interviews on a vast array of subjects, from an illustrous list of world-class grouches.
(007406—$17.00)

☐ **A CURMUDGEON'S GARDEN OF LOVE Compiled and Edited by Jon Winokur.** Romance, sex and love's myriad delusions—1,000 irreverent quotations, anecdotes, and interviews. Fun to peruse in solitude or to share with your current partner in crimes of the heart. (265517—$8.00)

☐ **FRIENDLY ADVICE Compiled and Edited by Jon Winokur.** A compendium of wise, witty and irreverent counsel. Take-it-or-leave-it pearls of wisdom spoken by those who've been hit too often by the slings and arrows of outrageous fortune . . . and who've just as often hit back. (267676—$9.00)

☐ **ZEN TO GO Compiled and Edited by Jon Winokur.** The Zen here is not confined to the East or to those who can twist themselves into the lotus position; rather it is open to anyone—as valid from the lips of athletes and artists as in the writings of sages and holy men. (265312—$9.95)

☐ **TRUE CONFESSIONS compiled and edited by Jon Winokur.** Shameless revelations, guilty pleasures, dreams, obsessions, and intimate secrets of the world's most famous people—in their own words. Quintessential reading for *People* people, National Enquirers—and all of us who want to know what the famous and infamous see when they look in a mirror. (270014—$8.00)

☐ **MONDO CANINE** *A Treasury of Quotations, Anecdotes, Essays, and Love in Celebration of Doggie Joie-De-Vivre* **Compiled and Edited by Jon Winokur.** From Emily Dickinson to Dave Barry, just about everyone has a waggish observation or a profound philosophical insight inspired by the world of dogs . . . Delightful reading and the perfect fit for anyone who's ever experienced the sublime companionship of a dog. (268516—$11.00)

Prices slightly higher in Canada.

Buy them at your local bookstore or use this convenient coupon for ordering.

PENGUIN USA
P.O. Box 999, Dept. #17109
Bergenfield, New Jersey 07621

Please send me the books I have checked above.
I am enclosing $＿＿＿＿＿＿＿＿＿＿＿ (please add $2.00 to cover postage and handling).
Send check or money order (no cash or C.O.D.'s) or charge by Mastercard or VISA (with a $15.00 minimum). Prices and numbers are subject to change without notice.

Card # ＿＿＿＿＿＿＿＿＿＿＿＿＿＿＿＿ Exp. Date ＿＿＿＿＿＿＿＿
Signature ＿＿＿＿＿＿＿＿＿＿＿＿＿＿＿＿＿＿＿＿＿＿＿
Name ＿＿＿＿＿＿＿＿＿＿＿＿＿＿＿＿＿＿＿＿＿＿＿＿
Address ＿＿＿＿＿＿＿＿＿＿＿＿＿＿＿＿＿＿＿＿＿＿
City ＿＿＿＿＿＿＿＿＿＿＿ State ＿＿＿＿＿ Zip Code ＿＿＿＿＿

For faster service when ordering by credit card call **1-800-253-6476**

Allow a minimum of 4-6 weeks for delivery. This offer is subject to change without notice